THE

ORIGIN AND EARLY HISTORY

OF

THE FAMILY OF POË OR POE

WITH FULL PEDIGREES OF THE IRISH BRANCH
OF THE FAMILY

AND

A DISCUSSION OF THE TRUE ANCESTRY OF EDGAR ALLAN POE,

THE AMERICAN POET

BY

SIR EDMUND THOMAS BEWLEY

M.A., LL D., F R.S.A.I.

Author of " The Bewleys of Cumberland," " The Family of Mulock," and other Works.

DUBLIN

PRINTED FOR THE AUTHOR

BY PONSONBY & GIBBS, AT THE UNIVERSITY PRESS

1906

TO

LIEUT.-COLONEL WILLIAM HUTCHESON POË, C.B., D.L.,

This little Book

IS DEDICATED AS A MARK OF ESTEEM AND REGARD

BY HIS SINCERE FRIEND

THE AUTHOR

PREFACE

G ENEALOGICAL problems have a great attraction for the genealogist. In the case of the family of Poë or Poe two problems of interest and difficulty presented themselves, viz., (1) the parentage and ancestry of William, Thomas, and Anthony Poe, who settled in Ireland early in the seventeenth century; and (2) the true ancestry of Edgar Allan Poe, the American poet; and it is submitted that correct solutions of both of them will be found in the following pages.

In starting on this two-fold quest, I was certainly free from any preconceived ideas, and, indeed, from any preliminary knowledge. As to the parentage and early ancestry of the Poe settlers, no tradition had been handed down in the family as to the locality from which William, Thomas, or Anthony Poe had come; and if they brought any documents with them from their former home, these must have been lost or destroyed so far back as the Rebellion of 1641. The legend of the German origin of the family, it will be seen, is a comparatively modern invention, and has no real foundation.

Finding a statement in " Burke's Landed Gentry of Ireland," that the Poe family was at one time settled in Yorkshire, I began my searches in that quarter, but they were without success. Amongst the vast number of wills proved in the Consistorial Court of York, there is not one of any testator bearing the name of Poe: the name is not met with in any of the Visitations or County Histories of Yorkshire; and a query of mine as to the Poe family, published in *Yorkshire Notes and Queries*, did not elicit any reply. The only connexion with the county that I was then able to discover was the residence for a time of James Poe, son of Dr. Leonard Poe, at Swindon Hall, in the Parish of Kirkby-Overblow.

As William Poe was described as of St. Edmund Bury (*i.e.* Bury St. Edmunds), Co. Suffolk, in the will of Sir Henry Mervyn, dated 29th May, 1646 (published in " Miscellanea Genealogica et Heraldica," vol. i, 2nd series, page 425), I next turned my attention to Suffolk, but could not find any further trace of the family in that county: It afterwards appeared, indeed, that it was only in his capacity of an officer in the Parliamentary Army that William Poe was quartered there.

On going through the numerous Reports of the Historical Manuscripts Commission, however, I came upon a document which ultimately turned out to be of great importance, viz., a list of the Officers of Sherwood Forest, in Nottinghamshire, of about the year 1591, now amongst the MSS. of the Duke of Rutland, at Belvoir Castle. In this Sir John Byron (father of the first Lord Byron) appeared as the Warden or Keeper of the Forest, and Richard Poe as Under-keeper. Searches in the Public Record Office, London, and elsewhere soon showed that there were numerous members of the family of Poe living in Nottinghamshire in the seventeenth century ; and when it appeared from the published State Papers that William Poe, of Manor Poe, Co. Fermanagh, was able to give the Commonwealth authorities important information respecting the private affairs of Sir John Byron, Lord Byron, of Newstead, Notts (son of the above-mentioned Sir John), it became pretty clear to me that he must have been one of the Nottinghamshire Poes. It was not, however, until more than a year afterwards, when having a search made amongst the Prerogative Court Wills, now in the Probate Registry at York, for the will (if any)

of James Poe, son of Dr. Leonard Poe, that the will turned up
of Anthony Poe, of Papplewick, Notts, the father of William,
Thomas, and Anthony Poe, and thus definitely settled the
question of their parentage.

The early ancestry of Edgar Allan Poe appeared for a long
time to be an insoluble puzzle. I, not unnaturally, expected
that some connexion would be found between the Poes of
Dring, County Cavan, from whom the poet was descended, and
the other Irish Poes. It will be seen, however, from the details
given in the chapter dealing specially with this subject, that
the true ancestry turned out to be different from what I had
anticipated, and that the solution was arrived at in a very
exceptional manner.

On reading the chapter relating to William Poe, many
persons may feel surprised that so much private family history
could be gathered from the Public Records , and a few of them
may appreciate the great interest and pleasure experienced in
hunting for information on a given subject in the Public
Records, and putting the items together afterwards in a connected narrative form. When I started on my work, absolutely
nothing was known about William Poe, save the bare fact that
he had been a Cromwellian Officer. In "Burke's Landed Gentry"
there were, no doubt, statements that he had served at the
Siege of Limerick, and had been rewarded for his military
services by a grant of lands in Ireland, which had been afterwards confirmed by William III ; but these statements were
erroneous, and had not a particle of foundation. The events
of his life recorded in this little volume have been ascertained
from Chancery Inquisitions, Ireland ; Patent Rolls and Fiants,
Ireland ; Communia Rolls, Ireland ; Bills in the Court of
Chancery in England ; Bills in the Court of Chancery in Ireland, and on the Equity Side of the Court of Exchequer,
Ireland ; Wills in the Probate Registry in England, and in the

Public Record Office, Dublin; Feet of Fines, Ireland; the published Calendars of State Papers, Ireland; the published Calendars of State Papers (Domestic), England; the Reports of the Historical Manuscripts Commission as to the Coke MSS., the House of Lords MSS., and the MSS. of the Duke of Manchester and of G. A. Lowndes, Esq.; the published Calendars of the Proceedings of the Committee for Advance of Money; and the Parish Register of St. Giles', Cripplegate, London. It need hardly be stated that for every printed volume or manuscript record in which information was found, scores were consulted with no useful result; and that for other portions of this work my researches had to take a much wider range.

In pursuing my inquiries I found a kindly disposition to help in all quarters. To Lieut.-Colonel William Hutcheson Poë, C.B., of Heywood, Queen's County, my special thanks are due. But for his encouragement and aid this little book might never have been published.

Several members of the family have helped to correct or supplement the recent portions of the pedigrees. I have had very interesting correspondence with Mrs. E. D. Latta, of Dilworth, Charlotte, N. C.; Miss Amelia FitzGerald Poe, of Baltimore, Md.; and G. O. Seilhamer, Esq., of Chambersburg, Pa., who most willingly contributed any information that they possessed bearing on the ancestry of Edgar Allan Poe.

The Rev. William Ball Wright, M.A., of Osbaldwick Vicarage, York, whose works are well known to Irish genealogists, rendered me important service in making numerous searches for me in the Probate Registry at York, and sending me abstracts of the documents found there. W. W. Glenny, Esq., of Barking, Essex, was good enough to furnish me with a copy of Susanna Bastwick's pathetic appeal to Parliament, taken from a little volume of petitions in the British Museum. To the Rev. John Standish, M.A., of Scarrington Vicarage, Notts;

Thomas M Blagg, Esq., of Newark-on-Trent, Notts ;
Rev. Thomas Warren, of Norwood ; Rev. Robert Leech, of
Drumlane, Co. Cavan ; Rev. J. H. Whitsitt, of Killeshandra,
Co. Cavan ; Rev. Albert E. Kay, of Kildallon Rectory, Co.
Cavan ; and Tenison Groves, Esq., of Blackrock, Co. Dublin,
I desire also to express my obligations.

EDMUND T. BEWLEY.

40, FITZWILLIAM PLACE,
     DUBLIN,
          September, 1906.

CONTENTS

—◆—

CONTENTS

THE FAMILY OF POË OR POE

I.

NO serious attempt has hitherto been made to investigate the origin and early history of the family of Poë or Poe. "Burke's Landed Gentry" has given currency to an alleged statement that the family came from the Upper Palatinate of the Rhine ; and this has been repeated in the "Dictionary of National Biography" in the notice of Dr. Leonard Poe, Physician to James I and Charles I. But the editor of the "Landed Gentry" is in no way responsible for this statement, which appears to be founded on no better authority than that of some unscrupulous pedigree-monger, who a great many years ago provided a too credulous member of the Poe family with a lineage, partly inaccurate and partly fictitious.[1]

Edgar Allan Poe, the American poet, believed that the Poe family was remotely of German origin ; and in an unpublished letter, dated 14th July, 1839, written to his cousin, George W. Poe, of Mobile, Alabama, he states :—

> "There can be no doubt, I think, that our family is originally German, as the name indicates it ; it is frequently met with in German works on Natural History, and a Mr. Poe is now living in Vienna, who has much reputation as a naturalist. The name there is spelled with an accent—thus, Poé—and is pronounced in two syllables—*Po-a*. As far back, however, as we can trace, our immediate progenitors are Irish."[2]

---

[1] See p. 69, *post*.

[2] I am indebted for a copy of this letter to Mrs. E. D. Latta, of Dilworth, Charlotte, North Carolina, whose maternal grandmother was a member of the American branch of the Poe Family.—E. T. B.

B

There is a family of Poe of German origin at present settled in the United States, whose ancestor, George Jacob Poe, emigrated from Germany to Maryland prior to 1742. To this family belonged General Orlando Metcalfe Poe, who was distinguished for his services on the Northern side in the Civil War, 1861-1865.[1]

But identity of name does not necessarily imply identity of stock ; and that families in both England and Germany bore the name of Poe seems merely an accidental coincidence.

It is indeed highly improbable that the English Poes could have been descended from any German family of that name.

In pre-Elizabethan times immigration from Germany must have been very rare ; and Germans coming to England were generally either engaged in commerce, or specially distinguished in some art or craft. These would naturally settle in London or in one of the large seaport towns. Aliens could not then acquire land ; and about the last place in England in which a German would be likely to be found located in those early times would be a country district in an inland county. But the first Poes of whom any records have hitherto been found in England were substantial yeomen, living in rural parishes and other places in Nottinghamshire and Derbyshire, giving to their children ordinary English names, and, so far as can be judged from their wills, of an ordinary English type. The parishes of Gedling, Hoveringham, Bingham, and Papplewick ; the towns of Nottingham and Newark; and Sherwood Forest are amongst the localities in Nottinghamshire in which they dwelt.

William Poo (Poe), of Horringham (Hoveringham), made his will, dated 15th July, 1557 (*i.e.* in the third year of the reign of Philip and Mary), and after giving 3*s.* 4*d.* (*i.e.* a half noble) to the church of Horringham, and another sum of 3*s.* 4*d.* to the church of Gedling, he made certain bequests to his sons Richard, Edmond, and Thomas, his wife Alice, and his daughters Joan and Alice, and his grandson Richard, son of Richard, the testator's son; and he appointed his wife and his children

---

[1] A pedigree of this family will be found in the " Kittochtinny Magazine," vol. i, p. 192, published at Chambersburg, Pennsylvania, and edited by the experienced genealogist, Mr. G. O. Seilhamer.

Thomas and Alice executors, and his special friend Richard Cliffe, of Lincoln, supervisor of his will.

Richard Poo (Poe), of Horringham, son of the last-mentioned William Poe, made his will, dated 31st May, 1564 ; and his wife Margaret and his only child Richard were the principal legatees. His wife was to make a dinner for the poor neighbours, and 5s. worth of bread was to be given to the poor who came to pray for his soul's health.

Amongst the MSS. of the Duke of Rutland at Belvoir Castle is a list of the officers of the Forest of Sherwood, to which the date of 1591 has been ascribed.[1]

In this are found the following entries :—

> " NEWSTEAD.　Sir John Byron.
> 　　Under-keeper, Richard Poe.
>
> ．　．　．　．　．　．　．　．
> " BLYDEWORTH.　Sir John Byron.
> 　　Under-keeper, Richard Poe."

This Sir John Byron, of Newstead, Notts, was father of the first Lord Byron. The Byrons had been stewards and wardens of the Forest of Sherwood from 1485 ; and the Manor of Papplewick, which was in the neighbourhood of Newstead, and adjoined the Forest, was granted to Sir John Byron (father of the Sir John mentioned in the foregoing list) and his heirs, by Letters Patent, dated 28th May, 32 Henry VIII (1540).

Amongst the tenants of the Manor of Papplewick, in January, 1605/6, was Anthony Poe, yeoman. He was the father of five sons, three of whom, viz., William, Thomas, and Anthony, settled in Ireland in connexion with the Plantation of Ulster, and afterwards served with distinction in the Parliamentary Army. William, the eldest son, settled in the County Tyrone, and afterwards resided for some time at Derrymore, in the County Fermanagh, to which he gave the name of Manor Poe. He attained the rank of Major in the Parliamentary Army in England ; and details of portion of his eventful life will be found further on. Thomas, the third son, settled in the County Fermanagh. He became a Lieutenant in the Parliamentary

---

[1] Twelfth Report of Historical MSS. Commission, App. ; MSS. of the Duke of Rutland, vol. i, p. 294.

Army in Ireland, and was the progenitor of the Tipperary
branch of the Poe family with all its ramifications. Anthony,
the fifth son, settled in the County Tyrone, and was afterwards
a Captain in the Parliamentary Army, both in England and
Ireland. He was the founder of a branch of the family long
seated in the County Louth.

But further notice of Anthony Poe, of Papplewick, and his
family must be reserved until brief reference has been made to
some other Nottinghamshire and Derbyshire Poes, and some
account has been given of Anthony Poe's kinsman, Dr. Leonard
Poe.

The entries of marriages in a large number of Nottinghamshire Parish Registers have been published by Mr. W. P. W.
Phillimore ;[1] and amongst them are found the following, relating
to members of the Poe family, taken from the Registers of the
Parish of Newark-upon-Trent :—

> " 10th December, 1609, William Poa (*sic*) and Bridget Wagstaff.
> " 20th October, 1611, Thomas Poa (*sic*) and Mary Moore.
> " 9th June, 1631, Richard Poe and Mary Laurence.
> " 9th May, 1723, John Hutcheson and Frances Poe."

The first two of these entries are interesting, as showing
that at this period the surname of the Nottinghamshire Poes
was pronounced as a dissyllable, in the same manner as that
of the Irish Poes is generally pronounced at the present day.
At St. Mary's, Nottingham, the following marriages are
recorded :—

> " 28th March, 1654, Robert Marson, of Peeter's Parish, and
> Isabel, daughter to Simon Poe.
> " 21st July, 1661, William Disney and Sarah Poy."

And at Bingham :—

> " 19th June, 1604, Thomas Poo and Benet Gyll.
> " 29th April, 1630, Miles Peeke and Elizabeth Poe."

Other evidence as to the existence of members of the Poe

---

[1] Unfortunately, the volumes are not indexed, and Poe entries can only
be discovered by going through them page by page, or examining the
entries relating to particular localities where Poes were likely to be met
with.

family in Nottinghamshire about this period is afforded by
Chancery pleadings, and Hearth-money Rolls, in the Public
Record Office, London

Gedling is a parish in the southern division of the
Wapentake of Thurgarton, and County of Nottingham, situate
within a few miles of Nottingham. On the 28th December,
1630, George Poe, of Gedling, yeoman, son and heir of Anne
Poe, his late mother, deceased, and Robert Gargrave, of Shelford,
son and heir of Alice Gargrave, his late mother, deceased, filed
a bill in Chancery to establish their title to certain messuages,
houses, and lands in the Minories, London, to which they were
entitled as heirs of Anne Poe and Alice Gargrave.

On the 1st May, 1668, Simon Poe,[1] senior, of the town and
County of Nottingham, cordwainer, filed his bill in the Court of
Chancery for the purpose of recovering possession of a messuage,
house, or tenement in Gedling, which the plaintiff's father,
Robert Poe, had been seised of in fee-tail, but from which the
plaintiff had been excluded by his younger brother, George Poe,
of Gedling, aided by Richard Kemp, of Gedling, and Mary
his wife. The bill also sought to recover a legacy left to the
plaintiff by one George Poe, of Gedling, son of Edward Poe, of
Gedling, the plaintiff's near kinsman.

A Hearth-money Roll of 15 Charles II (1663) of the
hundreds of Thurgarton and Lee, and of Newark and the town
of Newark, shows that in Gedling George Poe was assessed for
a house with one hearth ; and in Newark, Stodman Street,
Richard Poe was assessed for a house with two hearths, and
Margaret Poe for a house with one.

As to Derbyshire, we find that Richard Poe, of Ilkeston,
made his will, dated 3rd February, 1580, whereby, like his
namesake of Horringham, Notts, he directed that at his burial
his neighbours were to have a dinner, and further bequeathed a
penny to every person who attended his funeral.

On the 28th August, 1627, John Poe, of Wirksworth, in the
same county, was granted a certificate of innocency of a charge
cognisable by the ecclesiastical authorities.

---

[1] The freedoms granted by the Skinners' Company in 1689 include
"John Poe, son of Simon; patrimony." Miscell. Gen. et Herald., 3rd
series, vol. iii, p. 73.

In a Muster of the County of Derby held in 1638 the name of John Poe, of Bonsall, appears.[1]

The funeral certificate of Dr. Leonard Poe states that he was a grandson of Richard Poe, of Poesfeld, in the County of Derby; and as the latter must have been born at the beginning of the sixteenth century, he appears to be the earliest member of the Poe family of whom we have any certain knowledge.

In Yorkshire we learn that "Edeth, child of Bryan Poe, of the Forge," was baptized at Headingley, on 10th May, 1637;[2] and in the course of the seventeenth century an occasional reference occurs in some other parts of England to persons bearing the name of Poe.

The earliest records, however, of any Poes are found, as already stated, in Nottinghamshire and Derbyshire; and in Nottinghamshire also the name was most frequently met with.

The question as to the origin of the surname will be dealt with at a later stage, when it will be submitted that the cradle of the race must be sought elsewhere than in Germany.

---

[1] State Papers temp. Charles I, vol. ccccv, in the Public Record Office, London.

[2] Registers of Leeds Parish Church, published by Thoresby Society.

II.

DR. LEONARD POE : HIS ANCESTRY : HIS MEDICAL CAREER :
HIS FAMILY : HIS WILL.

THE eminent physician, Leonard Poe, was a kinsman, and
probably a nephew, of Anthony Poe, of Papplewick. From his
funeral certificate of record in the College of Arms, London, we
learn that he was a son of James Poe, who was a son of Richard
Poe, of Poesfeld, in the County of Derby.

Nothing definite is known as to his early life. He acquired
great skill as a physician without having had any orthodox
medical education, and in 1590 he was one of the physicians of the
celebrated and ill-fated Robert, Earl of Essex. The Earl, being
anxious to legalize the position of his *protégé* as a practitioner,
applied to the College of Physicians in May, 1590, to admit him
as a member, but the College refused to do so.[1] However, on
28th February, 1591, an order was made by the Privy Council
—no doubt by the influence of Essex—granting Leonard Poe
permission to practise,[2] and ultimately, on the 13th July, 1596,
he received the licence of the College at the instance of Essex.[3]

On the 30th June, 1598,[4] an order was made by the College
that Poe should be imprisoned and deprived of his licence, but
it was found subsequently that he had a letter of protection
from the Privy Council, and could not be imprisoned ; and the
matter between the College and Poe was referred to the arbitra-
tion of seven persons appointed by the Council. In pursuance
of the arbitrators' decision, Poe acknowledged the censure of
the College to be just, and paid a fine of five marks ; and, having
given security for his good behaviour in future, he was thereafter permitted to practise without molestation.

Some time after the accession of James I he became one of

---

[1] Eighth Report Histor. MSS. Com., App. ; MSS. of the College of
Physicians, p. 228.

[2] Acts of the Privy Council, 1591-2, p. 294.

[3] Eighth Report Histor. MSS. Com., App. ; MSS. of the College of
Physicians, p. 228.   [4] *Ibid.*

the Physicians to the Household ,[1] and in order to improve his position, his friends, Lords Northampton, Worcester, Salisbury, and Suffolk applied to the College of Physicians on the 26th June, 1609, that he might be chosen a Fellow of the College ; but the College flatly declined, on the ground of Poe's insufficient education.[2]   However, still more powerful influence was brought to work, and on the 9th July, 1609, he was admitted a Fellow.[3]

Dr. Leonard Poe was appointed one of the seven physicians of Charles I ;[4] and his name appears from time to time in the State Papers as attending on persons of distinction.

He had married, some time before the end of the reign of Queen Elizabeth,[5] Dionisia Boone, of the County of Sussex, by whom he had issue three sons and six daughters. His eldest son, Leonard, appears to have been *non compos mentis*. James, his second son, became a Fellow of King's College, Cambridge, and a Master of Arts of the University, and lived for some time with his wife Julian or Jane,[6] at Swindon Hall, Kirkby-Overblow, Yorkshire. Their daughter, Anne, was married on the 1st January, 1660/1, to Thomas Jenner, of the Inner Temple, afterwards Sir Thomas Jenner, a Baron of the Exchequer.[7] Dr. Leonard Poe's third son, Theophilus, matriculated from Broadgate Hall, Oxford, on 6th February, 1623/4 ; but he did not proceed to a degree, and is described in his father's will as " of unthriftie livinge."

Jane, the eldest daughter, married John Hankinson, of Totteridge, in the County of Hertford. Elizabeth, the second daughter, and Mary, the third daughter, died unmarried. Susanna, the fourth daughter, married Dr. John Bastwick, of Writtle, Essex, and afterwards of Colchester, in the same county ; and they had two daughters, Dionisia and Judith. He, unfortunately, incurred the resentment of Archbishop Laud by his vigorous writings against Prelacy ; and he was not only heavily

---

[1] Calendar of State Papers (Domestic), 1603–1610, p. 485.

[2] Eighth Report Histor. MSS. Com., App. ; MSS. of the College of Physicians, p. 228.   [3] *Ibid.*

[4] Twelfth Report Histor. MSS. Com., App. ; Coke MSS , vol. 1, p. 292.

[5] See a letter from Mrs. Dionise Poe to the Secretaries of the Earl of Essex, dated " Sunday, 1598 ": Histor. MSS. Com. Rep. ; Cecil MSS., part viii, p 560.

[6] As to her parentage, see Appendix A, *post.*

[7] For the licence for this marriage see Marriage Licences, Faculty Office, Harl. Soc., vol. xxiv, p. 48.

fined and imprisoned, but was put in the pillory, and had his ears
cut off by the common hangman. His brave wife went with
him to the pillory, gave him a hearty kiss at the foot of the
scaffold, and carried away his ears afterwards. The Doctor, it
is said, told the executioner to cut off the ears closely, that he
might not, like Prynne, have the chance of undergoing a second
operation. At Laud's instance he was imprisoned in the Scilly
Islands, where his wife could neither see him nor communicate
with him. When he was eventually released, he had lost every-
thing—his practice at Colchester, his hearing, and his estate.

After his death his widow presented a touching petition to
Parliament, in October, 1654, in which, after a long statement of
the sufferings of her husband, she says :—

> "Your Petitioner is made exceedingly miserable, and now, in
> the winter of her age, is comfortless, helpless, left indebted, and
> reduced to want and poverty ; that unless your Honours do her
> speedy and impartial justice, she and her poor children are like
> inevitably to perish. . . . . . . She is now aged, weak, and sickly.
>
> "That by the death of her dear husband she is deprived of all
> ways and means to get a subsistence. That as poverty is very grievous
> to all, so it is extremely bitter to those who have lived in plenty.
> That she has been for many years (and now in a more special
> manner is) a woman of sorrows, and all her hopes of future comfort
> in this life wholly depend upon your doing her justice."[1]

A sum of £5000 was granted to her by Parliament.

Judith, the fifth daughter of Dr. Leonard Poe, married
Thomas Grent, Doctor of Physic ; and Frances, the sixth
daughter, married David Ramsey, Page of the Bedchamber to
James I and Charles I, and had two children, William and
Frances Ramsey.[2]

Dr. Leonard Poe made his will, dated 18th February,
1630/1, and he thereby ordained and made his well-beloved
son, Mr. James Poe, being then a Master of Arts and Fellow
of King's College, Cambridge, his sole executor, upon the
condition that he should be bound unto the overseers in the
sum of £8000 for the due performance of the testator's will.

As touching the provision for the testator's son, Theophilus
Poe, the testator declared that in regard to his present unthrifty

---

[1] See small volume of petitions in British Museum, 669 f. 19 (28).
[2] For a remarkable incident in the life of David Ramsey, see p. 25, *post*.

living he should have paid unto him during his life £30 per annum, unless by God's grace he should thereafter reform himself to live and demean himself as became a sober, Christian, and temperate man; which if he should so do, and the executor and overseers should so find of him, they should lay out for him £500, and the annuity should cease.

All lands and tenements held by the testator in mortgage at his decease were to be sold, and the proceeds applied as directed by the will. The testator's lease of the Rectory of Ringwood, County Southampton, was to be renewed by the executor, James Poe, to whom the testator left it. The lease of the testator's dwellinghouse and its contents were to be sold.

If the testator's son, James Poe, should refuse to give the bond to the overseers, then he should only have the Rectory of Ringwood and £800, which should be paid him by the testator's son-in-law, Mr. David Ramsey, and his friend Mr. Walter Hillary, of Clifford's Inn, London, gent., whom then, and not before or otherwise, the testator ordained sole executors. £5 apiece was to be paid to them for their pains and labour. But if the testator's said son acted as executor, then they, together with Sir Walter Pye, Knight, Sir Thomas Merry, Knight, one of His Majesty's servants, "Mr. Manley, Esquire," another of His Majesty's servants, and Joseph Lane, of Fetter-lane, near Fleet-street, London, gent., should be overseers, and should receive £3 apiece for their care and pains.

If the testator's son, Leonard Poe, should become *compos mentis*, and the testator should not place him in some fit place to gain a competent means of living, he should have £700; but if he were not *compos mentis*, then £50 per annum should be paid for his maintenance.

The testator bequeathed to his daughter, Mrs. Grent, £100 for herself and her husband, because they had no children. To his two little grandchildren, William Ramsey and Frances Ramsey, he gave £100 each, to be paid them at twenty-one years of age or day of marriage with consent of their friends, whichever should first happen, the interest until then to be used by the testator's son-in-law for their education and maintenance.

To his grandchildren, Dionisia Bastwick and Judith Bastwick, the daughters of his son-in-law and daughter Bastwick, the testator gave £100 each, on the same conditions as the Ramsey legacies.

To his nephew, Robert Poe (being then an apprentice unto one Mr. Harris, a shoemaker in London), the testator gave £10, to be paid to him at the end of his apprenticeship.[1]

The testator then gave various small pecuniary legacies to friends and servants, including a sum of 40s. to his son-in-law, Mr. John Hankinson, to make him a ring; and bequeathed a sum of £5 to the poor of the parish of Christ Church, London, if he should die in that parish, or if not, to the poor of the parish in which he should die.

He gave a sum of £5 to his sister Beverley, or if she were dead to her eldest daughter. He also gave unto his loving brother, Anthony Poe, the sum of £10, and to the testator's cousin, William Poe, dwelling with one Richard Holman, gent., the sum of £10.

If his other sons should die leaving no issue, their legacies should lapse to his son James Poe; and if all died without issue, then to his daughters for their children. The residue of his estate he bequeathed to his son James Poe, his legacies, debts, and funeral expenses being paid, or if he were not executor, then to the testator's executors, to distribute amongst his children and grandchildren.

Dr. Leonard Poe died in February or March, 1630/1,[2] and was buried in Christ Church, London. His funeral certificate, which contains a good deal of important information, was duly recorded in the College of Arms, London, and a copy of it will be found in Appendix A, *post*.

His will was proved in the Prerogative Court of Canterbury on the 25th March, 1630/1, by his son James Poe, the sole executor.

The testator's cousin, William Poe, named as a legatee in his will, appears to have been William Poe, of the County Fermanagh, who, at the date of the will, was in London, looking for justice or Royal favour.

Dr. Leonard Poe's sons seem to have died without leaving male issue, and this branch of the Poe family became extinct.

---

[1] Probably Robert Poe, of Gedling, father of Simon Poe, senior, cordwainer, the plaintiff in the bill in Chancery of 1st May, 1668, mentioned at p. 5, *ante*.

[2] The writer of the article on Dr. Leonard Poe in the "Dictionary of National Biography" erroneously states that he died on the 4th April, 1631. This was, in fact, the date at which his Fellowship in the College of Physicians was filled up by the appointment of a successor.

III.

ALTHOUGH strict proof of the relationship cannot be given, it appears almost certain that Anthony Poe, of Papplewick, was a son of Richard Poe, of Poesfeld, Derbyshire, and a brother of James Poe, Dr. Leonard Poe's father, and of Richard Poe, the under-keeper of Sherwood Forest. It will be seen afterwards, from a letter of David Ramsey, that Anthony Poe's son William was undoubtedly a kinsman of Ramsey's wife Frances, who was a daughter of Dr. Leonard Poe; and, as already noted, William Poe is referred to as a cousin in Dr. Leonard Poe's will. James Poe, Dr. Leonard Poe's second son, seems also to be named as a cousin in the will of Anthony Poe, of Skreen, County Meath, another son of Anthony Poe, of Papplewick. That Dr. Leonard Poe had a brother named Anthony, and that Richard was a family name with Anthony Poe, of Papplewick and his descendants, are also circumstances of importance tending to support the views above expressed.

From the language of the grant of probate of the will of Anthony Poe, of Papplewick, we learn that his wife's maiden-name was Alice Frost. He had five sons, viz., William, John, Thomas, Richard, and Anthony; and three daughters, Alice, Anne, and Elizabeth. The last is not mentioned in her father's will, and perhaps was born after it was executed.[1]

The will is in the following terms:—

    "In the name of God. Amen. The ffifth daie of Januarie in the yeare of the raigne of oᵣ Souᵣaigne Lord James by the grace of God Kinge of England Scotland ffraunce and Ireland Defender of the faythe &c. viz: of England ffraunce and Ireland the third and of Scotland the nyne and thirtieth annoq: Dñi 1605.

    "I Anthonie Poe of Paplewick in the County of Nottingham, yeoman, being sicke in bodie, but of good and perfect remembrance,

---

[1] She is named in the will of her brother William Poe. See p. 35, *post.*

thanks be unto Almightie God for the same, do constitute ordaine & make this my present last Will & Testament in manner and forme following, revoking and disannullinge all former Wills & Testaments whatsoever at any tyme heretofore by me made or intended.

"ffirst I give and bequeath my soule unto Almightie God my Creator, faithfully beleeving in him that the same shalbe saved by the meritts and passion of oᵣ Lord Jesus Christ, and that he will place yt in heaven amongst the elected and heavenly Angels; and my bodie to the earth whereof it came, to be buryed in the south porch of the Church of Paplewicke aforesayde. Item. My mortuarie to be payde according to lawe. Item. I give and bequeath unto Ales Poe now my wyfe all that my lease & tearme of yeares yet to come & unexpyred of land in my now dwellinge house, w'thall and singuler thappurtenances to the same belonginge or in any wyse appertayninge, as I now have & inioye the same, duringe all the whole tyme of her widowhoode, keepinge her in my name. But if yᵗ shall fortune that the sayde Ales now my wyfe shall marie again with another man at any tyme before the lease & tearme of yeares be fully expyred and ended, then my Will is, and by these I do bequeath the Remainder and Residue of the saide lease & tearme of yeares of my sayde house w'thall and singular thappurtenances unto John Poe my second sonne & his assigns for & duringe the whole terme of yeares then to come and unexpyred. Provided always and neverthelesse my will is that the sayde John Poe my sonne shall pay or cause to be payde unto Willᵐ Poe my eldest sonne the some of fforty shillings of lawful monie of my londs w'thin two yeares next after his entreing into the sayde lease or terme of yeares in full satisfaction of all his childe's p'te or portion of goodes. And also I do give and bequeath unto Thomas Poe, Richard Poe, and Anthony Poe, my younger sonnes, every of them, twenty shillings of like lawful mony of England, to be like wyse payde unto every of them within two yeares next after his entrance into the sayde lease by my sayde sonne John Poe. Provyded further and neverthelesse my will is that if Ales Poe now my wyfe do not marie duringe all the tyme and terme of yeares yet to come in my sayde lease but do hold and inioye the same, as I have before given and bequeathed unto her, then my will is that the sayde Ales shall pay the sayde some of ffive poundes unto my sayde foure sonnes, as is afforesayde, and that the sayde Ales now my wyfe shall suffer my sayde sonne John Poe to have and inioye one whole yeare of the last of the sayde terme, that then he the sayde John Poe may be in full possession of all the sayde premisses & so in possibility to be thereof tenant and obtaine a new lease. Also I give and bequeath unto my sayde sonne John Poe ffoure yeardes of greene cloath to make him a suite of, beinge now in my house readie, & my sword and my dagger. Also I give and bequeath

unto my sayde sonne John Poe my great table with all formes &
seates to the same belonging, and one paire of great cobyrons, one
spitt, the best, w'thall iron hookes and gallowe irons belonginge,
unto my sonne Willm Poe one peece of blew cloath, beinge a yarde
an a halfe, and my blew coote, & other five sheep like the rest. I
give & bequeath unto my sonne John Poe my buffe lether hoose. I
give & bequeath unto Ales Poe my daughter my new cubbord &
eight peaces of pewter of the best all, savinge one great charger, &
one bedsteade wth a trundle bedd where I now do lye, wth two good
coverleds & one blanckett & one fetherbedd, beinge my worst, w^th
bolster and a pillow to the same bedd belonginge, and one seeled
chest & my best brass pot & one chafinge Dish & my best candlesticke, & five sheepe to be set owte by my supervis'rs. I give &
bequeath unto my daughter Anne Poe one other bedsteade, busett
up, being fellow to y^t, and eight peeces of pewter equall to thother,
and my best fetherbedd with one boulster, one pillow, & one of the
best coverings & one blankitt, and my old cupbord and my second
brasse pot, and five shepe equall to the rest, and one great chest
beinge the best but one, & one candlesticke, being fellow to her
sister's. Item. I give unto the sayde Anne my Landyron and the
iron gates belonginge to the same. Item. I give & bequeath unto
my sonne Anthonie Poe one bullock calfe and five sheepe to be sett
out by my Supervisors equall to the rest. Item. I give & bequeath
unto my sonne Thomas five sheepe to be set out as is afforesayde.
Item. I give & bequeath unto Richard my sonne other five sheepe
to be sett out as is aforesayde. All the rest of my goodes, debts,
cattels, chattells moveable and immoveable not before given &
bequeathed, my debts, legacies & funerall expences beinge fully
discharged, I give & bequeath them unto Ales Poe now my wyffe,
whome I do make and appointe full & sole executrix of this my
present last Will & Testament. And I do desyre my good frendes
Bryan Patten & Robt Aussabancke to be Supervisors of this my last
Will & Testament, and I do give & bequeath unto either of them
for theyr paynes to be taken therein the some of ii^s vi^d to be payde
unto them by my sayde executrix. Also my will is that whereas I
have before in this my present last Will & Testament given &
bequeathed certain sheepe to my children therein above named,
that if y^t shall please God to take me out of this life before the next
clippinge tyme then the sayde sheepe shall be devyded & severally
marked to the use of my sayde children to goe forward to their best
profitt, savinge the sheepe given to my youngest sonnes, whereof I
will & by these presents do appoint that Ales my wyfe shall take the
profitt of the wolle towards fyndinge of their apparell, so long as she
keepeth herself widow. In witness whereof I have hereunto sett
my hand & seale the day and yeare first above written. These
beinge witnesses. Thomas Hutchinson, John Watson, James
Cheever."

The testator died some time in or prior to the year 1612, and on the 8th October, 1612, probate of his will was duly granted by the Prerogative Court of York to his widow and relict, Alice Poe, otherwise Frost.

Anthony Poe no doubt perceived that his eldest son William was of a roving, adventurous disposition, and not likely to settle down quietly in Papplewick. He treated his second son John, therefore, as his probable successor in his farm.

The Plantation of Ulster early in the seventeenth century offered great attractions to energetic young Englishmen of the yeoman or gentleman farmer class. Manors of 2000, 1500, and 1000 acres had been created, subject to a condition that the English or Scotch grantees should plant them with British Protestants ; and the latter could obtain fee-farm grants and leases of long tenure on most favourable terms.

William Poe and his brothers Thomas and Anthony were tempted by these attractions, and became settlers in two of these newly created manors. But the life and adventures of William Poe merit separate treatment.

IV.

WILLIAM POE: SETTLEMENT IN COUNTY TYRONE: MARRIAGE
WITH FRANCES SEDBOROUGH: PROCEEDINGS IN CON-
NEXION WITH SEDBOROUGH ESTATE: APPLICATIONS FOR
ROYAL LETTERS: IMPRISONMENT: MILITARY SERVICE IN
ENGLAND: ATTEMPT TO RECOVER SEDBOROUGH ESTATE:
HIS WILL.

ONE of the original undertakers—as they were called—in the
Plantation of the County Tyrone was Sir Mervyn Tuchet,
who was allotted "the great proportion of Brade," containing
2000 acres. His interest became subsequently vested in Sir
Henry Mervyn, Lieutenant-General and Admiral of His
Majesty's Navy in the Narrow Seas, who after a time conveyed
the lands to his son, Captain James Mervyn.

William Poe acquired from Captain James Mervyn an
interest either in fee-simple or fee-farm of five balliboes or
townlands in "the great proportion of Brade"; and his
connexion with the lands is shown in the following manner.
The undertaker and his assigns were in this case bound not to
let more than one-fourth of the lands to "the meere Irish"; and
by an inquisition[1] taken in the County Tyrone on the 29th May,
1632, it was found amongst other things that Bryan O'Neal and
others, "meere Irish," held by demise from William Poe, assignee
unto James Mervyn, the ballibo of land called Mullavinny, in
excess of the portion that might be lawfully let.

It does not seem to have been treated as forfeited, as
William Poe levied a fine of the five balliboes more than forty
years afterwards.

In 1628 William Poe married his first wife, Frances, only
daughter of John Sedborough, of Mount Sedborough, County
Fermanagh.[2] There appears to have been issue of the marriage

---

[1] Calendar of Chancery Inquisitions (Ulster), Tyrone, No. 35, Charles I.
[2] See Chancery Bill, Mary Poe v. John Maine & Others, filed 20 Jan.,
1685.

an only child, Frances, who married, first, a member of the Kemp family, and became the mother of William Kemp referred to—as will be afterwards seen—in the will of William Poe. Kemp is a name found at this time at Gedling, and elsewhere in Nottinghamshire, and Frances Poe would appear to have taken a husband from the neighbourhood of her father's old home. She married, secondly, James Percy, Esq., of whom nothing is at present known.

This Sedborough marriage had such an important bearing on the subsequent career of William Poe, that, in order to explain the course of events, it is necessary to give some account of the family and property of John Sedborough.

He seems to have been a member of the family of Sedborough, seated for some generations at Porlock, in Somersetshire, and was one of the original undertakers in the Plantation of Ulster.

He was allotted the lands known as "the small proportion of Latgir," otherwise Latgare, in the precinct of Clancally (now Clankelly), and County Fermanagh, which were duly conveyed to him by Letters Patent, dated 12th May, 11 James I (1613).

In the Plantation of Ulster, the allotments to the undertakers were termed respectively "great, middle, or small proportions," according as they comprised 2000, 1500, or 1000 acres of land; and the grant to John Sedborough included, in addition to Latgir or Latgare (now Loughgare), twenty-two other denominations or townlands, which, with Latgir, made up approximately 1000 acres.[1] One of these denominations—which requires special notice—was Derrymore, situate in the parish of Clones. By the Letters Patent, the Manor of Mount Sedborough was created, and John Sedborough was given the customary manorial rights; but the grant was made subject, amongst others, to the condition, that if John Sedborough, his heirs, or assigns, should alien or demise the lands or any part thereof to any person or persons being "mere Irish," or to any other person or persons, who within one year before such alienation or demise had not taken the oath of supremacy, the Letters Patent, as to the parts of the premises so aliened or demised, should be void and of no effect in law.

John Sedborough had by his first marriage an only son, Peter Sedborough, who on reaching man's estate married

---

[1] Patent Rolls, 11 James I, part 1, m. 69.

C

Frances, daughter of Sir Edmond Fettiplace, of Gloucestershire, and had by her an only daughter, Barbara by name. John Sedborough married secondly a wife named Elinor, and there was issue of this marriage a daughter Frances, who, as already stated, was married to William Poe in 1628.

Peter Sedborough having died in the lifetime of his father, the latter by a deed, dated 10th March, 15 James I (1617/8), granted to Frances Sedborough, the widow of Peter, and Barbara Sedborough, the daughter and heiress of Peter, the Manor of Mount Sedborough, *alias* Latgare, to hold to Frances for her life, and then to Barbara and the heirs of her body, reserving, however, to John Sedborough and Elinor his wife an interest for their lives in the entire of the Manor and lands.

John Sedborough died soon after William Poe's marriage to Frances Sedborough; and it would seem that on the occasion of this marriage he made over to William Poe the lands of Derrymore, which, as already stated, formed portion of the Manor of Mount Sedborough. William Poe was certainly in possession of these lands shortly after John Sedborough's death, and held them under the name of "Manor Poe" during his lifetime.

Undertakers in the Plantation of Ulster had found it almost impossible, in many cases, to comply strictly with the condition inserted in the Letters Patent that no alienation or demise should be made to any of the native Irish; and the original Letters Patent were frequently surrendered for the purpose of obtaining less stringent terms. On payment of a fine of £30, and undertaking to pay double the rent originally reserved, a re-grant was made, almost as a matter of course, with such a modification of the condition as to alienation as would enable the undertaker to make alienations or lettings to the native Irish to the extent of one-fourth of the lands.

In many instances undertakers, or those deriving under them, had neglected to see that their grantees or lessees had taken the oath of supremacy; and it is not surprising to find that the condition as to alienation contained in the Sedborough Patent had not been always observed.

But when William Poe became aware, about the time of John Sedborough's death, that there had been a violation of this condition in the patent, it occurred to him—in an evil hour—that he would take advantage of it, and would endeavour to obtain a grant from the Crown of such of the lands as should appear to have been forfeited.

Very possibly the absence of any suitable provision for his wife Frances Poe, and the settlement that John Sedborough had made of the Mount Sedborough estate in 1617/8, may have influenced his conduct.

In Michaelmas Term, 1628, William Poe sued out of the Court of Chancery a Commission addressed to certain Commissioners therein named, requiring them to inquire, with the aid of a jury, as to what breaches, if any, there had been of the condition as to alienation contained in the Letters Patent to John Sedborough. His professed object was to discover whether any disloyal subjects were in possession of lands that properly belonged to the Crown; but his real object was to obtain for himself a grant of the forfeited lands.

Amongst those likely to be affected by William Poe's proceedings were Stephen Allen, Esq., and Robert Allen— probably a near relative—who were sub-tenants of portions of the Mount Sedborough estate, and either through inadvertence or otherwise had not taken the oath of supremacy. Stephen Allen was a man of some position in the County Fermanagh.[1] He was often selected by the authorities as one of the Commissioners for holding inquisitions in the county, and he had held the important post of Attorney-General for Ulster from June, 1617.[2] If William Poe had known or appreciated that the effect of his proceedings would be to impeach or challenge Stephen Allen's title to portion of Mount Sedborough, he might well have hesitated before applying for the Commission.

Stephen Allen probably thought that the best parry to William Poe's attack was a thrust; and accordingly he, and several of the other tenants or sub-tenants of the estate, joined in indicting Poe for what was then known as the offence of *common barratry*.

In the bill of indictment William Poe, described as of Derrymore, in the County of Fermanagh, yeoman, was charged as

---

[1] In MS. No. 672 (F. 3. 15), in the Library of Trinity College, Dublin, the name of Stephen Allen appears in both the County Louth and County Fermanagh in a list of persons who already held, or were fit to hold, the Commission of the Peace.

[2] "Liber Munerum Publicorum Hiberniae," vol. i, part ii, p. 193.

being a barrator[1] and public disturber of the peace, and an oppressor and calumniator of the King's subjects, and a stirrer-up of strife amongst them.[2]   The case came on for trial at the Assizes for the County Fermanagh held in the spring of 1628/9, and William Poe was duly acquitted by the jury. Notwithstanding this, Stephen Allen succeeded in preferring a fresh charge against him for the same offence, and got him bound over by recognizance in the sum of £100 to stand his trial at the next Summer Assizes.[3]

Distrusting apparently the result of a second trial, William Poe made his way to England to seek Royal protection and favour.

In a petition presented to the King he stated that he had in last Michaelmas Term sued forth a Commission to inquire after the possessions concealed from the King in the County Fermanagh, but had been hindered from executing it by Stephen Allen, Thomas Turner, Hugh Stokes, Thomas Sergeant, Bryan McDonell, and Toby Vesey, who were dis-loyal subjects ; that they persecuted him with lawsuits, and cost him money ; and he prayed that if these accusers did not prove their charges, they might be compelled to pay the petitioner's costs, and be committed to prison until they found sureties for good behaviour.[4]

On this an order was made on the 14th July, 1629, "that the King orders letters to the effect of this petition to be written to the Lord Deputy."

But to obtain the King's Letter necessary to carry this order into effect was a matter that required time, influence, and money ; and, as will be seen presently, the letter was not actually procured until March, 1629/30.

In the meantime the Assizes for Fermanagh were held at Enniskillen on 27th August, 1629, and William Poe, being detained in England by contrary winds, did not appear. His trial on the charge made by the Allens had consequently to be

---

[1] In legal phraseology this means "one who vexatiously raises, or incites to, litigation "; "one who, from maliciousness or for the sake of gain, raises discord between neighbours."

[2] S. P. (Ir.), Add., 1625–1660, p. 133.

[3] *Ibid.*, p. 142 ; Communia Rolls, M. T., 1630, in the Public Record Office, Dublin.

[4] S. P. (Ir.), 1625–1632, p. 464.

postponed, and his recognizance for £100 was forfeited, and was directed to be estreated.[1]

He petitioned for a respite of proceedings, and the prayer of his petition was acceded to by a King's Letter, dated 31st December, 1629, upon which an order was made by the Lords Justices for Ireland on 27th April, 1630, staying the proceedings.[2]

There is no record of any inquisition having been taken under the Commission sued out by William Poe; but, anticipating its findings, he had made preparations for a re-grant of the Mount Sedborough estate to himself. Amongst the State Papers of September, 1629, is found the docket or minute of a grant to be made to William Poe of the small proportion of Latgir (or Latgare), in the County Fermanagh, containing 1,000 acres, for which he was to give security to pay the Vice-Treasurer of Ireland £30 as a fine, and £11 6s. 8d. rent, instead of the former rent of £5 6s. 8d.[3]

On the 22nd December, 1629, a fresh Commission was issued out of Chancery, directed to Sir Stephen Butler and the other Commissioners therein named, to investigate the breaches of the condition as to alienation contained in the Sedborough Patent.[4]

The inquisition[5] in pursuance of this Commission was taken at Newtown, *alias* Castlecoole, in the County Fermanagh, on the 20th January, 1629/30, and it found that from time to time the condition as to alienation had been violated either by John Sedborough or those claiming under him in the instances particularly set out. In some cases lettings for one year or for a few months had been made to some of the "mere Irish," and in other cases tenants of John Sedborough, or of persons deriving under him, had not taken the oath of supremacy. But almost all the

---

[1] S. P. (Ir.), Add., 1625–1660, p. 142.

[2] Communia Rolls, M. T., 1630, in the Public Record Office, Dublin. The respite was granted in the first instance until the next Assizes, viz. the Spring Assizes of 1629/30, but it was afterwards extended to the Summer Assizes of 1630.   [3] S. P. (Ir.), 1625–1632, p. 480.

[4] The original Commission is attached to the inquisition taken under it, now in the Public Record Office, Dublin.

[5] The inquisition is No. 13 of those taken in Fermanagh in the reign of Charles I; but in the printed Calendar of Chancery Inquisitions (Ulster), Fermanagh, it erroneously appears as No. 55, and the inquisition which should be No. 55 is printed as No. 13.

lands included in the Patent had been at one time or another the subject of some illegal or irregular demise or alienation ; and if the conditions of the Patent were strictly enforced, these lands would have been forfeited to the Crown. It is important to notice—having regard to William Poe's conduct more than forty years afterwards—that the inquisition set out the particulars of the deed of the 10th March, 15 James I (1617/8), before mentioned, executed by John Sedborough in favour of his daughter-in-law, Frances Sedborough, and his granddaughter, Barbara.

Amongst the breaches of the condition as to alienation found by the inquisition was a grant in fee by John Sedborough to Ralph Daye of the denomination of Cornemuckle, and a subsequent grant by the latter to Stephen Allen, neither of whom had taken the oath of supremacy.

But after the inquisition was taken, and before it was returned into Chancery, either Stephen Allen, or the friends of Barbara Sedborough, the heir-at-law of John Sedborough, succeeded in getting a re-grant of the lands made to trustees for Barbara Sedborough, and thus cut the ground from under William Poe's feet. By Letters Patent, dated 6th May, 1630, the " small proportion of Latgare " and the other lands included in the Sedborough Patent were granted in fee-simple to Robert, Lord Dillon, Baron of Kilkenny West, and Francis, Lord Mountnorris, in free and common socage, at the yearly rent of £10 13s. 4d., and were created the Manoi of Latgare, subject to the conditions and provisoes usual in grants to undertakers in the Plantation of the Province of Ulster.[1]

Though no trust was disclosed by the Letters Patent, the grantees, who occupied high positions, were in fact trustees for the heirs of John Sedborough, and were so found in an inquisition taken at Newtown, County Fermanagh, on 14th November, 1632.[2]

By an Inquisition *post mortem*, taken at Enniskillen, on the 9th September, 1639, it was found that John Sedborough had

---

[1] Patent Roll, 6 Charles I, part 4, *facie*, m. 1.

[2] Cal. Chancery Inquisitions (Ulster), Fermanagh, No. 33, Charles I. The Rev. George Hill, not having his attention called to this inquisition, supposed that Robert, Lord Dillon, and Francis, Lord Mountnorris, were beneficial owners under the Letters Patent of 6th May, 1630, and concluded that John Sedborough had sold his interest in the lands. See his " Plantation of Ulster," p. 482, n. (93).

died ten years past, and that at the time of his death he was seised of the small proportion of Latgare, containing by estimation 1000 acres : that his heir-at-law was his granddaughter Barbara, the daughter and heir of his son Peter Sedborough : that she was nineteen years of age at the date of her father's death, and unmarried, but had since married John Mayne. " The premises at the time of the death of the said John Sedborough were held, and now are held, of the King, as of his Castle at Dublin, in free and common socage, at the yearly rent of £10 13s. 4d."[1]

In March, 1629/30, through the intervention of Lord Dorchester, William Poe got Sir Sidney Montagu, Master of the Court of Requests, to submit to the King a letter to carry out the order of the 14th July, 1629, made on Poe's petition.

The letter, which bore date the 6th March, 1629/30, was duly signed by the King,[2] and was conveyed to William Poe through Sir Sidney Montagu ;[3] and by it Stephen and Robert Allen were directed to pay William Poe £50 for his expenses, in case they should not make good their charges against him. But such a letter without the Royal Seal attached would have no efficacy, and Poe was obliged to give a bribe to John Woodison, a clerk in the Signet Office, to get the King's Signet to the letter.[4] This was ultimately done, and the letter was transmitted to the authorities in Ireland.

The case against William Poe came on for trial on the 10th July, 1630, at the Fermanagh Assizes, and Poe was again duly acquitted by the jury.[5] An order was subsequently made that he should not be tried again on the same charges, and that any bonds he had given should be restored.[6]

The Allens, having been apprised of the King's Letter in favour of Poe, set to work to nullify it.

Stephen Allen, describing himself as " Attorney for Ulster," and the other persons who had been associated with him in the prosecution of William Poe, presented a petition[7] to the King, in which they stated, amongst other things, that, by virtue of the Royal Letter obtained by Poe, some of the petitioners were

---

[1] Cal. Chancery Inquisitions (Ulster), Fermanagh, No. 40, Charles I.
[2] S. P. (Ir.), 1625–1632, p. 612.   [3] *Ibid.*, p. 614.
[4] *Ibid.*, pp. 607, 612.   [5] *Ibid.*, p. 579.   [6] *Ibid.*, p. 583.   [7] *Ibid*, p. 578.

committed by Lord Balfour, Governor of the County Fermanagh, until, on petition to the Lords Justices, they gave sureties for £50 to answer Poe's charges. They submitted that they were able to prove the charges they had made against Poe; and as he probably used fraudulent means to get the Royal Letter, they asked that they might be discharged of their bonds, and that the Justices of the Peace in Fermanagh, Tyrone, and Armagh might be given orders to take evidence regarding Poe's life, carriage, and behaviour.

As a counterblast to this petition, a certificate[1] was signed by a large number of persons, defending Poe against the complaints made against him, and stating that Allen's charges were tried at Enniskillen Assizes on the 10th July last, and were found to be false ; and that Allen's hatred for him was based on the fact that he got a commission to inquire into certain Crown lands held by him (Allen). This certificate, which bore date the 22nd September, 1630, was signed by about fifty noblemen and gentlemen of the North of Ireland, including Lord Balfour, Br. Enniskillen,[2] Robert Dillon, Leo. Blennerhassett, Claud Hamilton, and Francis Caporne, Provost of Dungannon.

However, Stephen Allen and his associates succeeded in getting a letter from the King, recalling the letter previously given to William Poe, whom they represented as having forged the King's Privy Seal affixed to it.[3] The letter secured by Allen bore date the 16th October, 1630 ; and shortly after it had been issued, William Poe proceeded to London, and with the aid of his friends endeavoured to get a fresh King's Letter in his favour.[4]

Amongst those who interested themselves on William Poe's behalf was David Ramsey, Page or Gentleman of the Privy Chamber, who, it will be recollected, was married to a daughter of Dr. Leonard Poe. An investigation as to the genuineness of the letter obtained by William Poe was made by Mr. William Boswell, Secretary to the Lord Keeper. That it was duly signed by the King on the application of Sir Sidney Montagu appeared to be beyond question; but there was a suggestion that

---

[1] S. P. (Ir.), 1625–1632, p. 579.

[2] Bryan Maguire, cr. Baron Enniskillen, 1628 ; forfeited, 1644.

[3] S. P. (Ir.), 1625–1632, p. 612.   [4] *Ibid.*, p. 679.

the seal affixed to it might have been taken off some other letter.[1]

On the 15th January, 1630/1, Mr. Richard Berington—apparently a Secretary to Sir Sidney Montagu—wrote to Mr. David Ramsey as follows[2] :—

> " In March last Sir Sidney Montagu obtained a letter from the King on behalf of Mr. William Poe. I do not remember its addressee or contents."

And on the 19th July, 1631, Mr. David Ramsey wrote in the following terms to Sir John Coke, Principal Secretary of State to His Majesty :—

> "I beseech you, in the business of my wife's kinsman Poe, referred to Mr. Boswell (who saith he had no order thereon from the Lord Privy Seal and your honour), to the end that now, at last, he may get a despatch, after 8 months chargeable attendance, to his near beggary and utter ruin. Be pleased to draw up a certificate, according to the equity and justness of the cause as you find it."[3]

These letters are of genealogical importance, as showing that William Poe was a *kinsman* of David Ramsey's wife, daughter of Dr. Leonard Poe.[4]

---

[1] S. P. (Ir.), 1625–1632, p. 533 ; but there seem to be several errors in the dates as printed.

[2] S. P. (Ir.), 1625–1632, p. 598.

[3] Twelfth Report Histor. MSS. Com., App. ; Coke MSS., vol. i, p. 435.

[4] Within a few months after the date of this letter of David Ramsey, he was a defendant in a celebrated case in the Court of Chivalry (reported, "State Trials," vol. iii, p. 483), which excited great interest in London at the time Donald Lord Rea, a Scottish nobleman, accused Ramsey of high treason, and having no witness to support his charge, Ramsey, as he was entitled by law to do, offered to clear himself by combat; and this challenge was accepted by his accuser. A Court of Chivalry was then convened by order of a Commission under the Great Seal, and its proceedings, which extended over many months, were conducted with great pomp and ceremony. The Court fixed the 12th April, 1632, as the day for the duel, and assigned Tuthill Fields, Westminster, as the place where it was to be fought. Each of the combatants was to be entitled to have the following weapons : "A long sword, 4½ft. in length, hilt and all, in breadth 2 inches; short sword, 1 yard and 4 inches in length, hilt and all, in breadth 2 inches; pike, 15 ft. in length, head and all ; dagger, 19 inches in length, hilt and all, in breadth an inch." It is amusing to read that Ramsey petitioned that his counsel might be received into the lists or field

Sir William Balfour, Lieutenant of the Tower, was one of those who at the time exerted himself on William Poe's behalf, and wrote in his favour to Viscount Dorchester, Secretary of State.[1]

Amongst the State Papers of this period that have been preserved are draft letters of the King, prepared respectively in 1631 and 1632, in favour of William Poe, purporting to quash the letter obtained by Allen, and to grant to Poe the full right to inquire of all lands concealed from the King in Ireland by Allen and others, in Mayo, Fermanagh, and the adjoining counties; but they remained but drafts, and were never perfected.[2]

On the 13th May, 1633, William Poe wrote a letter to Humphrey Fulwood, secretary to Sir John Coke, stating that as Fulwood seemed discontented with a particular letter, the writer had drawn another, and begged him to get the King's hand to one of them; that he would have had an end of the business at the Council held more than a year ago, but for the persuasions of Fulwood and William Boswell; that he would be with him ere long, and bring what he promised.[3]

The last clause of this letter suggests that "palm-oil" was needed to smooth difficulties in matters of this kind.

But the King's Letter was not obtained; and William Poe returned to Ireland, baffled and disappointed.

On the 26th December, 1629, an agreement was entered into between William Poe and William Goodin, of the Parish of St. Clement Danes, County of Middlesex, tailor, whereby a limited partnership was constituted for the purchase of cattle in Ireland to be sold subsequently in England. In pursuance of this agreement William Poe purchased cattle in the North of Ireland,

---

with him, to counsel him what should be needful; but it is not surprising that he also applied to have "a chirurgeon, with his ointments and instruments, to serve and aid him when need required." The King, in the first instance, prorogued the day of combat from the 12th April to the 17th May, and then, by an arbitrary exercise of his prerogative, he dismissed the Court, discharged the combat, acquitted Ramsey of high treason, but at the same time rated him soundly for having "so often offended by his violent tongue."

[1] S. P. (Domestic), 1631–1633, p. 180.
[2] S. P (Ir.), 1625–1632, pp. 619, 679.
[3] S. P. (Domestic), 1633–1634, p. 56.

including a number from his brother, Thomas Poe, and shipped
them to an English port, from which they were driven slowly
through many English counties, and sold from time to time at
fairs and elsewhere.   But before they had been entirely disposed
of, disputes arose between the partners as to the number of
cattle originally purchased, and the profits made on the sales;
and on the 19th April, 1632, William Poe, described as of "the
Mannor of Poe, in the Parish of Clownes, in the County
ffearemanagh, within the Kingdom of Ireland, Esq.," filed a
Bill in the Court of Chancery in England against William
Goodin, for the purpose of winding up the partnership, and
having proper accounts taken of the partnership transactions.
The Chancery pleadings do not mention the port in Ireland from
which the cattle were shipped, nor the port in England at which
they were landed; but from sundry small details given, it would
seem that they were driven from the Counties of Tyrone and
Fermanagh to Dublin, and were sent from that to Bristol by
sea.   They left Ireland early in November, 1630, and had reached
Berkshire before the end of the month.   From thence they were
driven to Warwickshire, where some sales were made; and at the
end of May, 1631, some of them were sold at Banbury Fair, in
Oxfordshire.   The cattle appear to have been bought in Ireland
at an average price of £2 per head ; and some idea of the difficulties and perils incurred in driving them through Ireland may
be gathered from William Poe's statement that several of them
were worried and killed by *wolves*.

There is no information forthcoming as to how William Poe
spent the time between his return to Ireland and 1637.   But evil
days were coming for him, and for the country.   In 1637[1] he was
summoned to appear before the Star Chamber in London to
answer for misdemeanours and forgery; and having been arrested
in Ireland by order of the Lord Deputy, acting under instructions
from the English Privy Council, he was sent over to London for
trial.   The case appears to have come before the Star Chamber
in England on the 30th May, 1638, when Poe was found guilty
of procuring counterfeit persons to personate men of value in
sealing a bond of £200.   Whether this was connected in any
way with the Allens' case, it is impossible to say.[2]

---

[1] S. P. (Domestic), 1637, p. 49 ; S. P. (Ir.), 1633–1647, p. 158.

[2] S. P. (Domestic), 1637–1638, p. 473.

On the eve of his trial and immediately after it, he succeeded in raising some small sums of money on bills of exchange, which were the subject of litigation some years afterwards.[1]

With the approach of the Civil War, a new era dawned for William Poe. He presented a petition to Parliament in May, 1642, describing himself as a distressed prisoner in the King's Bench, and praying relief against an unjust sentence in the Star Chamber, obtained at the suit of Sir Edward Bullock. The latter, he alleged, notwithstanding the abolition of the Star Chamber, by combination with the Warden of the Fleet, prevented the petitioner's discharge; and on his procuring a writ of *habeas corpus*, committed him to the Fleet on an action for £200 under the judgment of the Star Chamber. He stated that he had lost all his estate and some of his dearest friends by the rebellion in Ireland, where he had served as a commander, and that he was ready for any further service; and he prayed for relief and enlargement.[2]

He was released shortly afterwards; and when the Civil War broke out, he entered the Parliamentary Army as a Captain. Where and when he had previously served in Ireland has not been ascertained.

Although it is not possible to follow his military career in detail, several matters connected with it can be gathered from the published State Papers and other sources.

He was placed in command of a troop of horse, and was under the control of that County Organization for mutual defence known as the "Eastern Association," which by Cromwell's indefatigable activity attained great efficiency. He had much to do with Suffolk, and gained the complete confidence of the Committee for Suffolk, established at Bury St. Edmunds. He appears, too, to have served in Cromwell's own regiment. Some account of his proceedings in the autumn of 1643 will be found in a report made by him to the Deputy-Lieutenants and Committee for the County of Essex, dated 19th August, 1643.[3]

---

[1] Answer of Lewis Morgan and John Saunders, sworn 22nd and 24th February, 1641, to bill of complaint of William Poe, in Public Record Office, London

[2] Fifth Report Histor. MSS. Com., App.; House of Lords MSS., p. 40.

[3] Seventh Report Histor. MSS. Com., App., MSS. of G. A. Lowndes, Esq., p. 559.

In February, 1644/5, the inhabitants of the County of Rutland, in a petition to the Earl of Manchester, Commander of the Parliamentary Army, suggested that the force under Captain Poe, then at Stamford, should be sent to their aid;[1] and shortly afterwards he distinguished himself at the Battle of Melton Mowbray.

In a letter dated 15th March, 1644/5, bearing six signatures, written from Bury St. Edmunds, and addressed to the Earl of Manchester, Captain William Poe was recommended "for encouragement by some considerable part of his pay now in arrear," on account of "his valorous carriage in the late fight at Melton Mowbray."[2]

Encouragement in the manner suggested he failed to get, owing to lack of funds.

In a communication from the Committee of both Houses, dated 3rd September, 1645, to Captain William Poe, he was directed to take command of 400 horse out of the forces supplied by the Eastern Association, and to proceed with them to Grantham.[3]

In the course of the following twelve months his troop appears to have suffered heavily, for when in 1646 Colonel Jones was appointed to take over the 400 horse from the Eastern Association at St. Albans, he reported amongst other things: "to which appeared Captain Poe his troop, consisting of a captain, a lieutenant, two trumpeters, and three soldiers, in all officers and soldiers to the number of seven."[4]

William Poe's first wife, Frances Sedborough, died not many years after their marriage; and he subsequently married a wife whose Christian name was Mary, and maiden name Jones. At the time of her marriage with William Poe, she was, it would appear, the widow of a knight, as in the entry of her burial at St. Giles', Cripplegate, London, she is called Lady Mary Poe; and in the Fine levied by William Poe and her in 1675, she is referred to as "*domina* Maria." The name of her first husband has not been ascertained. There was not any issue of this second marriage of William Poe.

Sir Henry Mervyn, of Westminster, Lieutenant-General and

[1] Eighth Report Histor. MSS. Com., App.; Duke of Manchester's MSS., p. 62.   [2] *Ibid.*   [3] S. P. (Domestic), 1645–1647, p. 109.
[4] S. P. (Ir.), 1633–1647, p. 475.

Admiral of His Majesty's Navy in the Narrow Seas, was, as already stated, the father of Captain James Mervyn, from whom William Poe had acquired part of "the great proportion of Brade," in the County Tyrone.

He made his will, dated 29th May, 1646, and thereby confirmed the deed of gift bearing even date with his will of £12,000, or thereabouts, "long since due to me from His Majesty," unto William Poe, of St. Edmund Bury, Co. Suffolk, and appointed him executor, "whom failing, my loving friend, Ellis Holmes, of Kensington, gentleman, to be executor, and entitled, subject to payment of debts, legacies, and funeral expenses, to the residue of my estate."[1]

Sir Henry Mervyn died shortly afterwards, and his will was proved in London on 12th June, 1646, by Ellis Holmes

It is not easy to conjecture why this £12,000 should have been made over by a deed of gift to William Poe. Under one of the provisions of the will he would have been absolutely entitled, after payment of the testator's debts, legacies, and funeral expenses, to so much of the remainder of the testator's estate as should be received by him during his life ; and, as he declined to act as executor, we may conclude that he looked on the gift as valueless.

In March, 1646/7, Captain William Poe offered to serve in Ireland, and presented a petition[2] to the House of Commons to the following effect :—

> "The petitioner faithfully executed the commands of the Parliament from the 21st February, 1642/3, until the 11th August, 1646, during which time he performed many great services. He has borrowed large sums of money to pay for his soldiers' quarters, and other necessaries, and there is now justly due to him and his officers 4495*l*. 18*s*. 10*d*.
>
> "On the 10th of December last, their Lordships ordered him to repair to the Committee for Suffolk, for examination and payment of his accounts ; this he has done, and the Committee have examined the same, but have certified that they have no money. He prays that what is due to him and his officers may be paid, in order that he may repay the money he has borrowed. He undertakes to raise three troops of horse, eighty in each troop, and bring them to the waterside at his own charge ; and if 1000*l*. more be advanced to him, he will raise two troops in Ireland within six months after his arrival."

---

[1] Miscel. Gen. et Herald., vol. 1, 2nd series, p. 425 ; P. C. C. 80 Twisse.
[2] Sixth Report Histor. MSS. Com., App. ; House of Lords MSS., p. 167.

'*Annexed*:

" 1. Copy of Certificate of the Committee for Suffolk of the amount due to Captain Poe.
" 2. Copy of further Certificate of the same Committee.
" 3. Copy of letter from the Committee of the Eastern Association to the House of Commons, testifying the good services performed by Captain Poe, 30th June, 1645.
" 4. Copy of letter from the Committee for Suffolk to the House of Commons, to the same effect as the preceding, 14th June, 1645.
" 5. Account of moneys due to Captain Wm. Poe, his officers and troopers, from the 10th February, 1644/5 (which day he passed his accounts), until the 9th April, 1645
" 6 Copy of the Order of the Commons for a petition of Captain Poe to be taken into consideration."

However, money to pay the arrears due to him was not forthcoming, and there was no means of accepting his offer to serve in Ireland.

He appears to have been engaged for some time after this on special service for the Committee of both Houses of Parliament. For example, in the Minutes of the Proceedings of the Committee of the 19th February, 1647/8, we find an order :—" That a warrant be directed to Captain William Poe to apprehend James Kendrick," and also an entry of the issue of this warrant to Captain William Poe and the Messengers of the Committee.[1]

In the interval between this and the following July he was promoted to the rank of Major, and in the Minutes of the Proceedings of the Committee of both Houses of the 5th July, 1648, there is an entry of a warrant to Major Poe to go with a party of horse to the river bank in order to seize a boat suspected to be laden with arms ; and an order " that Major Poe do bring hither the cloak-bag, and money which he took from Mr. Stafford."[2]

On the 11th October, 1648, Major William Poe, along with Colonels Anthony Hungerford and Moore, and Daniel Searle, made an information "that seven years ago Sir James Stonehouse bought of Sir John Byron, Lord Byron, of Newstead, County Notts (a delinquent), lands worth 1200*l.* a year ; that 9000*l.* or

---

[1] S. P. (Domestic), 1648-1649, p. 19.   [2] *Ibid.*, pp. 161, 162.

10,000l. of the purchase-money was unpaid. It was reported that he told a kinsman he owed the 10,000l., but was wiser than to pay it to Parliament."[1]

Prolonged investigations took place as to the amount due by Sir James Stonehouse to Lord Byron, and he was ultimately ordered to pay 3000l. As he failed to do so, a sequestrator was appointed over his estates, and small sums were levied from time to time, one-fourth of which was paid to each of the informers. The proceedings lasted for at least five years, and the amount that William Poe gained by the transaction cannot be determined.

William Poe, it will be recollected, spent his early years on the Byron estate at Papplewick, in the immediate neighbourhood of the seat of the Byron family at Newstead ; and we may feel sure that he gained his information as to Lord Byron's affairs from some of his relatives or friends in the locality.

Major William Poe was also concerned in giving information about the property of Colonel Richard Conquest,[2] a recusant, and Henry, Lord Herbert,[3] a delinquent ; but he does not appear to have derived much benefit thereby.

In or about the month of December, 1654, the following petition was presented by Colonel Humphrey Brewster and Major William Poe to the Protector and Council :—

"By Commissions from you, the Earl of Manchester, and Lord Grey of Wark (sic), Poe and his brother Anthony served faithfully in your regiment in the Associated Counties, as Captain and Lieutenant, from 21st February, 1642/3, to 19th April, 1646, in suppressing the malignants, and disbursed therein 3201l. 14s. 4d., as appears by order of Parliament of 10th December, 1646.

"Ant. Poe sold his share therein to Major William Poe, to whom 2601l. 19s. 6d. is also due, as executor of Captain John Birkbeck and Katherine, his wife   To Brewster 725l. 7s. 6d. is due for service in the wars.

"As God has seated you in the supreme power, to the great rejoicing of all who love the nation's prosperity, we—being frustrate of satisfaction other ways—beg an order to the Trustees at Worcester House, to pay as from the sale of four forests, on the

---

[1] Cal. of Proceedings of Committee for Advance of Money, part ii, p. 771.

[2] *Ibid.*, part iii, p. 1191.

[3] *Ibid.*, part i, pp. 209, 210.

Ordinance of 30th August, 1654, or from lands in the Cos. Dublin, Cork, Kildare, and Caterlaugh yet undisposed of, or from forfeited corporation lands, according to the Act of 26th September, 1653, for adventurers and soldiers, or from our own discoveries."[1]

No lands in the counties mentioned, or elsewhere in Ireland, were allotted to the petitioners ; and whether their claims were satisfied either wholly or partially in any other way cannot now be ascertained.[2]

No further mention of William Poe has been found in the published State Papers. He remained, however, in England, until June, 1673.[3]

Before leaving Ireland, in 1637, William Poe had appointed his brother, Thomas Poe, to act as his agent in Ireland ; and during his lengthened absence he remitted to him several sums of money to be held on his behalf. On his return to Ireland, an account was settled between him and his brother, and a sum of £448 10s. 1d. was admitted by Thomas to be due. In June, 1674, Thomas made a payment on account ; but the balance not having been paid, William brought an action for its recovery, and the proceedings were pending when William died, in 1678.[4]

Barbara Sedborough, the heiress-at-law of John Sedborough, had, as already stated, married John Mayne ; and after the death of Elinor, the widow of John Sedborough, she and her husband went into possession of the Manor of Mount Sedborough. They were residing there when the Rebellion broke out in October, 1641 : the Mansion-house was attacked, and all the farming stock and other movable chattel property carried off or destroyed ; and two or three days afterwards, when John Mayne and his wife were endeavouring to escape, they were pursued by a party of rebels, and he was murdered.[5] His

---

[1] S. P. (Domestic), 1654, p. 421.

[2] See a petition to Parliament of the same period, signed by William Poe and Anthony Poe, amongst others, in Appendix B, *post*.

[3] See statements to that effect in the bill filed by Mary Poe on the Equity Side of the Court of Exchequer, on 11th February, 1685, and in the bill filed by her in Chancery, on 20th January, 1685.

[4] Bill on Equity Side of the Exchequer, filed by Mary Poe on 11th February, 1685.

[5] See deposition of Barbara Maine, in the Examinations as to the Rebellion of 1641, amongst the MSS. in the Library of Trinity College, Dublin (F. 3. 6)

widow succeeded afterwards in making her way to Dublin along with her infant children, including John Mayne the younger, the eldest son and heir to the Mount Sedborough estate. He was educated in England; but when he grew up, he returned to Mount Sedborough, and was living there when William Poe returned to Ireland in 1673.

The title-deeds relating to many estates throughout Ireland had been burned or otherwise destroyed in the Rebellion of 1641; but it is astounding to find that William Poe had the temerity to bring an action of ejectment against John Mayne the younger, for recovery of the *entire* of the Mount Sedborough or Latgare estates, claiming, as it would appear, that they had been made over to him by John Sedborough at the time of his marriage, and that he had been possessed of them from that time until the breaking out of the Rebellion of 1641. The ejectment proceedings had not been brought to trial at the time of William Poe's death.

William Poe, described as of Manor Poe, in the parish of Clones and County of Fermanagh, made his will, dated 24th May, 1678, and thereby constituted his wife Mary Poe his only heiress and executrix, and devised and bequeathed to her all his real and personal estate, subject to the payment of his debts and legacies. He bequeathed to his grandchild William Kemp, 5s.; and to Robert Kemp, 5s.; to his brother Thomas Poe, 2s. 6d.; to his nephew Emanuel Poe, son of the said Thomas, 1s.; to his niece Mary Poore, daughter of the said Thomas, 2s. 6d.; to his nephew Thomas Poe, brother of the said Emanuel, 1s.; to his nephew Richard Poe, son to his said brother Thomas Poe, 5s.; and also to the said Richard Poe, when the testator's lands[1] should be recovered from Charles Belford and the heirs of Hugh, Lord Glanelly (*sic*),[2] ten tates of the said lands lying together, to him the said Richard and his heirs for ever, the said ten tates to be set out to the said Richard by the testator's said executrix at her discretion. To his cousin Francis Brassie and his wife, 10s. apiece; to Daniel Poe, Esq.,

---

[1] The lands referred to have not been identified. They were, no doubt, in the County Fermanagh, as a "tate" is a measure of land peculiar to the counties of Fermanagh and Monaghan. In the Plantation of Ulster it was treated as 30 acres; but the native Irish estimated it at 60 acres.

[2] Hugh Hamilton, cr. Lord Hamilton, Baron of Glenawly.

son to the testator's brother, Anthony Poe, 1*s.* ; to the testator's sister-in-law, his mother, 2*s* 6*d.* ; to Sarah Holland, Ann Sterling, and Mary Mackaleire, daughters to the testator's said brother, Anthony Poe, 2*s.* 6*d.* apiece ; to the testator's niece, Ann Hide, daughter to the testator's brother, John Poe, and Ann, her daughter, 2*s.* apiece ; to the testator's brother-in-law, Charles Bastard,[1] who was married to his sister Elizabeth Poe, and to Adam Bastard, his son, 5*s.* apiece.[2]

The testator died shortly afterwards, and his will was proved by his widow and executrix, Mary Poe, in the Prerogative Court, Ireland, on the 8th December, 1682, and in the Prerogative Court of Canterbury, on the 10th February, 1686/7.

Mary Poe, the second wife of William Poe, was a party with him to a fine of his Tyrone estate, levied in Michaelmas Term, 1675,[3] in which, as already mentioned, she is described as "*domina* Maria," or "Lady Mary." On the 11th February, 1685, she filed a bill on the Equity side of the Court of Exchequer in Ireland against William Poe, a grandson of Thomas Poe, and Edward Plaistead, joint executors of Thomas Poe, deceased, for an account of the moneys received by him as agent for Major William Poe ; but as no further proceedings were taken, the case must have been settled.[4]

She also attempted to prosecute William Poe's claim to the Mount Sedborough or Latgare estates, and for that purpose filed a bill in Chancery, on the 20th January, 1685, against John Mayne and others. But the claim was as hopeless as it was unmeritorious. William Poe's assertion that he was in possession of the estate from his marriage until the Rebellion of 1641, was quite inconsistent with the findings of the Inquisition *post mortem* of the 9th September, 1639 ;[5] and his whole case was shattered by the deed of the 10th March, 1617/8, which,

---

[1] He also was an assignee of part of Captain James Mervyn's interest in the great proportion of Brade (see Cal. Chancery Inquisitions (Ulster), Tyrone, No. 35, Charles I), and he was Captain over the Muster for the Barony of Omagh, Co. Tyrone (S. P , Ir., 1616–1625, p. 229).

[2] Exemplification of will of William Poe, in Public Record Office, Dublin.

[3] Feet of Fines, M.T., 27 Charles II, in the Public Record Office, Dublin.

[4] Bill in the Equity Exchequer, entered 11th February, 1685, now in the Public Record Office, Dublin.

[5] See p. 22, *ante.*

though lost, was recited in the Inquisition of the 20th January, 1629/30.[1]

One can only hope that he was in his dotage when he put forward this wild and impossible claim.

The Mount Sedborough estate was retained by John Mayne, who was the progenitor of the Maynes, long seated at Freame Mount and Glynch House, County Monaghan.[2]

Mary Poe, the widow of William Poe, died in September, 1688, intestate, and was buried on the 20th of that month at St. Giles', Cripplegate, London. In the Parish Register her burial is entered thus: "The Lady Mary Poe, relict to William Poe, Esquire to ye King's Body, viz. to King Charles ye first and King Charles ye second: bur. 20 September, 1688." No evidence has been obtained that William Poe held any such post under either of the Sovereigns named.

On the 2nd October, 1688, letters of administration of the goods of Mary Poe, late of the parish of St. Giles', Cripplegate, widow, were granted by the Prerogative Court of Canterbury to Frances Percy, otherwise Kemp. otherwise Poe (the wife of James Percy, Esq.), a creditor of the deceased, Elinor Alexander, a grand-niece of the deceased on her brother's side, and her next-of-kin, having renounced her rights; and on the 6th August, 1690, further letters of administration of the goods of Mary Poe, otherwise Jones, late of the parish of St. Giles', Cripplegate, widow, were granted by the same court to Sarah Jones, the cousin once removed of the deceased, on the revocation of the prior grant made to Frances Percy, otherwise Kemp, otherwise Poe.

Such is the history of William Poe as disclosed by the public records and other documents above referred to; and we now turn to his brother Thomas.

---

[1] See p. 21, *ante.*

[2] Amongst the best-known members of this family were the Hon. Edward Mayne, one of the Justices of the Common Pleas and afterwards of the King's Bench in Ireland; and Sir Richard Mayne, K.C.B., for many years Chief Commissioner of the Metropolitan Police, London.

V.

THOMAS POE: SETTLEMENT IN COUNTY FERMANAGH. SERVICE IN THE PARLIAMENTARY ARMY IN IRELAND: GRANT OF LANDS IN COUNTY TIPPERARY: HIS WILL

THOMAS POE, the third son of Anthony Poe, of Papplewick, came to Ireland about the same time as his brother William, and settled as a tenant on portion of the lands of Edernagh, in the County Fermanagh, of which Thomas Blenerhassett was the undertaker in the Plantation of Ulster.[1] Sir Leonard Blenerhassett, a son of this Thomas Blenerhassett, and eventually his successor at Edernagh, married Deborah Mervyn, a sister of Captain James Mervyn, from whom William Poe acquired part of " the great proportion of Brade," in the County Tyrone ; and one may conjecture that it was through some connexion or friendship with the Mervyn family that William and Thomas Poe, and—as will be seen presently—their brother Anthony, were led to settle in Ireland.

The undertakers in the Plantation of Ulster were bound to supply arms for their tenants and retainers; and official musters were held from time to time, at which the names of those appearing, and the nature of their equipment, were duly noted.

In a Muster Roll of Ulster,[2] which, from internal evidence, appears to refer to the year 1630, or thereabouts, we find in the portion relating to the County Fermanagh :—

> " MR. LEONARD BLENERHASSETT.
> Undertaker of 2000 acres :
> Barony of Lourg.
> The names of his men and arms.
> No. 1. Thomas Poe. Sword and snaphance."[3]

---

[1] Cal. Chancery Inquisitions (Ulster), Fermanagh, No. 2, Charles I ; Rev. George Hill's " Plantation of Ulster," p. 489.

[2] Add. MSS. No. 4770, in British Museum.

[3] A *snaphance* was a hand-gun, or a pistol, made to be fired by flint and steel.

Thomas Poe was extensively engaged in raising cattle for sale in Dublin, and, at times at least, for export to England.[1]

When an army was raised to put down the great Rebellion that broke out in October, 1641, Thomas Poe took service in it, and served as a Lieutenant until the insurrection was suppressed. At the outbreak of the Rebellion he suffered much from the plundering of the rebels, the total amount of his losses being estimated at £3360—a very large sum in those days.

He resided afterwards for some time in the County Donegal; and in the deposition[2] which he made on the 19th September, 1643, for the purpose of proving the injuries sustained by him, he is described as " Thomas Poe, of Killeene, in the County of Donegal, Esq." In a bill in Chancery, filed by him on the 2nd December, in the same year, against Daniel Hutchinson, of Dublin, for the recovery of a debt, his address is given as " Donegal, in the County of Donegal."

When the allotment of lands to the soldiers and adventurers came to be made, he duly established his claim; and by Letters Patent, dated 2nd March, 20 Charles II (1667/8), the lands of Killownine, containing 115a. or. 9p. profitable land and 62a. unprofitable land; part of Cappagh West, called Lislane, containing 16a. profitable land and 5a. unprofitable land; and part of Knockgilty-granane, containing 88a. 1r. 29p. profitable land and 70a. unprofitable land (making altogether 355a. 2r. 5p., statute measure), situate in the barony of Upper Ormond, and County of Tipperary, were granted to Thomas Poe, in fee-simple, subject to the yearly quit-rent of £3 7s.[3]

Thomas Poe acquired also, by purchase, the several lands in the barony of Lower Ormond mentioned in his will, which were held by him in fee-simple.

Thomas Poe made his will, dated 19th December, 35 Chas. II (1683)—being then resident at Cloghan, King's County—and thereby gave to his son, Richard Poe, and his heirs for ever, one

---

[1] See bill in Chancery against Daniel Hutchinson, referred to *infra*, and pleadings in the Chancery suit of William Poe *v.* William Goodin, mentioned at p. 26, *supra*.

[2] Examinations as to the Rebellion of 1641, amongst the MSS. in the Library of Trinity College, Dublin, F. 3. 10. f. 138.

[3] Patent Rolls, 20 Charles II, part 2, *dorso*, m. 23, in the Public Record Office, Dublin.

moiety of Belline, Clonmuck, and Coolahallagagh, in the barony of Lower Ormond, and Parish of Nenagh, in the County of Tipperary, containing 382 a., plantation measure ; and he gave the other moiety to his grandson, Thomas Poe, the fourth son of his son, Emanuel Poe, to be enjoyed from the age of fifteen, and then to him and his heirs for ever ; if he died under age, or without issue, then to Emanuel Poe, the second son of his son, Emanuel, with remainder to James Poe, the third son of the said Emanuel, with remainder to Joseph Poe, the fifth son of the said Emanuel Poe.

To William Poe, the eldest son of the said Emanuel Poe, he gave fourscore pounds ; to Emanuel Poe, the second son of the said Emanuel, £30; and similar bequests were made to James Poe, the third son, Thomas Poe, the fourth son, and Joseph Poe, the fifth son of the said Emanuel Poe.

To Elinor Poe, the youngest daughter of his said son, Emanuel Poe, he gave £30, at her age of eighteen, or marriage. He gave legacies of £10 each to Elizabeth Poe, the eldest daughter ; Arabella, the second daughter ; Jane, the third daughter ; and Mary, the youngest daughter of his son Richard Poe.

To Thomas Poe, the eldest son of his son Richard Poe, he gave £5 ; and similar legacies of £5 each to Edward, the second son ; John, the third son ; Anthony, the fourth son ; Richard, the fifth son; William, the sixth son ; and Robert, the seventh son of the testator's son Richard Poe. To Nicholas Bond, son of Nicholas Bond by the testator's daughter, Mary Poe, he gave £20.

He gave to Mary Poe, *alias* Hill, the widow and relict of the testator's son, Emanuel Poe, £5 ; to his daughter, Eleanor Bracye, *alias* Poe, £10 ; and to his son, Thomas Poe, £10.

He appointed his grandson, William Poe, and Edward Playstead, executors, and his son, Thomas Poe, and Richard Allen, of Killenarden, County Tipperary, Supervisors of his said will.[1]

The testator died shortly afterwards, and his will was proved by the executors, William Poe and Edward Playstead, in the Consistorial Court of Killaloe.

The particulars as to the descendants of Thomas Poe,

---

[1] Original will amongst the documents from the Consistorial Court of Killaloe, in the Public Record Office, Dublin.

appearing in Pedigrees A and B, *post*, have been obtained by the examination of a very large number of wills, memorials of deeds, entries in parish registers, census returns, marriage licence bonds, bills in Chancery, and in the Equity Exchequer, and other documents, supplemented by information given by some of the present members of the Poe family.

VI

ANTHONY POE : SETTLEMENT IN THE COUNTY TYRONE : MILITARY SERVICE IN ENGLAND AND IRELAND : HIS WILL : GRANT OF LANDS IN THE COUNTY LOUTH TO HIS WIDOW, MARY POE, AND HIS SON, DANIEL POE.

ANTHONY POE seems to have come to Ireland about the same time as William, and, like him, settled on the Mervyn estate, in the County Tyrone. In the Muster Roll of Ulster,[1] already mentioned, to which the date 1630 is attributed, we find :—

    " Co. of Tyrone. Omy (Omagh) Barony.

" CAPTAIN MERVIN, undertaker of 6000 acres : his men and arms :

.   .   .   .

" No. 47, Edward Poe, sword and pike.

.   .   .   .   .   .

" No. 50, Anthony Poe, no arms."

Of Anthony Poe's doings, between this and the breaking out of the Civil War in England, we know nothing. He served for many years in the Parliamentary Army in England as a Lieutenant, but having attained the rank of Captain, he was sent over to Ireland to take part in the suppression of the Rebellion or Civil War there. By an order of the Committee of Lords and Commons, at Derby House, for Irish Affairs, dated 14th April, 1648, Captain Anthony Poe was to carry over 150 men to Derry on the terms given to Colonel Wetton.[2] From other entries in the State Papers relating to Colonel Wetton, it appears that he was to advance the necessary moneys for the pay and maintenance of his men, being content to be paid out of the Excise of Leinster, though this service would yield nothing for some time, being allowed 8 per cent. interest.

Captain Anthony Poe, it will be remembered, sold his arrears of English pay, or portion of them, to his brother William,[3] so that, no doubt, he was not without funds to start with.

---

[1] Add. MSS. No. 4770, in British Museum.

[2] S. P. (Ir.), 1625–1660, Addenda, p. 778.   [3] Page 32, *ante.*

Anthony Poe served with the army in Ireland until the end of the Rebellion, and became entitled to the benefit of the Ordinance, dated 27th September, 1653, " for the satisfaction of the Adventurers for Lands in Ireland, and the Arrears of the Soldiery there."

He died, however, many years before the Cromwellian Settlement of Ireland was carried out ; and on the expiration of his military service he took to farming, and was residing on his farm at Skreen, in the County Meath, at the time of his death.

He married a wife whose Christian name was Mary, and they had six children, viz. . two sons, Daniel and Anthony, and four daughters, Sara, Anne, Elizabeth, and Mary.

He made his will, dated 10th January, 1653, and thereby bequeathed to his wife, Mary Poe, portion of his farming stock and a third part of his household stuff. He gave other portions of his farming stock to each of his daughters, Sara, Anne, and Elizabeth ; to his son Daniel Poe other portion of his farming stock, and the two-thirds part of all the lands and houses that he then had or thereafter should have from the State, Commonwealth, or Keepers of England. He also gave to his son Anthony other portion of his farming stock, and one-third part of all the lands and houses that he then had or thereafter should have from the State, Commonwealth, or Keepers of England. All his houses, gardens, and parks that he had in and about Drogheda he gave towards the maintaining of the house and the children in clothes ; and his wife was to have the disposing of it as long as she kept the testator's name or lived a widow, and then Sara Poe and Anne Poe were to have the disposing of it for the use of the little children, till Daniel Poe or Anthony Poe came to age. His wife was to have the third part of all the lands that he then had or thereafter should have, as long as she bore his name or lived a widow, and no longer. He gave such part of his arrears as was due to him in England to his daughter Mary Poe, at the discretion of his brother William Poe, and the rest to be divided between Daniel Poe and Anthony Poe. " One-half of the plough and corn to my wife, and the other half to my daughters, Sara Poe and Anne Poe, to be equally divided betwixt them, and soe they are to continue as long as they shall live together." He appointed his wife, Mary Poe, and his daughter, Anne Poe, his executors ; and he appointed his daughter, Sara Poe, his brother, Thomas Poe, his cousin, Manuel Poe, and his cousin, James Poe, his overseers, to see this his last will and testament performed.[1]

On the death of the testator the will was proved in Dublin, on the 12th May, 1654, by Mary Poe, widow, and Anne Poe, the executors.

At the time this will was made the term "cousin" was very often used to denote any near relative, including a nephew or niece,[2] and the testator's "cousin, Manuel Poe," was without doubt, his nephew, Emanuel Poe, son of his brother Thomas. James Poe, also named as one of the overseers of the will, was probably James, the eldest son of Dr. Leonard Poe.

When the Court of Claims sat to ascertain the lands to which the soldiers and adventurers were entitled, a claim in respect of Captain Anthony Poe, deceased, was established by Mary Poe, his widow, and Daniel Poe, his eldest son and heir-at-law ; and by Letters Patent, dated 18th June, 19 Charles II (1667), portions of the lands of Dromgooldstown, lying on the north side of the river of Atherdee (Ardee), containing 104a. 3r. plantation measure, and in Athelint, out of the northerly part, 171a. 3r. (making together 447a. 3r. 22p. statute measure), situate in the Barony of Atherdee (Ardee) and County of Louth, were granted in fee-simple to Mary and Daniel Poe, subject to the yearly quit-rent of £5 11s. 11½d.[3] By further Letters Patent, dated 24th March, 22 Charles II (1669/70), a further portion of the lands of Dromgooldstown, containing 48a. 2r. 15p. statute measure, situate in the Parish of Stabannon, Barony of Atherdee (Ardee), and County of Louth, were granted in fee-simple to Mary Poe, widow of Anthony Poe, subject to the yearly quit-rent of 12s. 1¾d.[4]

The descendants of Anthony Poe will be found in Pedigree A, *post*, so far as it was possible to ascertain them from

---

[1] Original will in the Public Record Office, Dublin.

[2] For example, in the will of William Poe (p. 34, *ante*) the testator's "*cousin* Francis Brassie and his wife" denoted his niece Eleanor Bressy and her husband.

[3] Patent Rolls, 19 Charles II, part 8, *facie*, m. 46, in the Public Record Office, Dublin.

[4] Patent Rolls, 22 Charles II, part 3, *facie*, m. 6, in the Public Record Office, Dublin.

public records; but the members of this branch of the Poes were not in the habit of making wills, or if any were made, they or many of them remained unproved. Hence the pedigree given may be in some respects defective.

The lands comprised in the grants from the Crown of 1667 and 1669/70, or some of them, appear to have been known for many years as "Poe's Court"; but having been heavily incumbered by successive owners—after the fashion of the times—all the lands were sold in a Chancery suit instituted by a mortgagee, by a bill filed on the 16th November, 1780.[1]

It has not been found possible to trace this line of the Poes later than James Poe, of Dublin, born in 1772, and his brothers Anthony, George, and Samuel Jackson Poe; but it seems probable that all of them died without issue.

Though the name of Daniel Poe's wife is not known, there are grounds for believing that she was a member of the Townley family, of the County Louth. Samuel was a Christian name used at the time in the Townley family. Daniel Poe's eldest son was named Samuel; and the latter executed a post-nuptial settlement,[2] dated 16th March, 1708, in which the trustees were Hamilton Townley and Richard Tisdall. Elinor Poe, the wife of Samuel Poe, had very probably been a Tisdall.

On 24th November, 1680, Daniel Poe received a pardon for killing Ralph Wallis;[3] and in 1684/5 he was a lieutenant in the Earl of Mount Alexander's Company of the Earl of Arran's Regiment of Horse.[4]

---

[1] The decree for sale is dated 30th May, 1783.
[2] Memorial in Registry of Deeds Office.
[3] Patent Rolls, 32 Charles II, part 2, f.
[4] Histor. MSS. Com. Rep., Ormonde MSS., vol. II, p. 226.

VII.

JOHN POE : RICHARD POE : EDWARD POE : ANNE POE, WIDOW.

OUR only knowledge of John Poe, the second son of Anthony Poe, of Papplewick, is derived from his father's will, and the will of his brother, Major William Poe. The provisions of his father's will show that his father was desirous that John should be absolutely entitled to the interest in the Papplewick holding in the event of his wife, Anne Poe, marrying again during the subsisting term of the lease ; and that in case his wife remained a widow, she should make over the possession of the holding to John during the last year of the term, so that he might have what is known as the tenant-right of occupation, and be in a favourable position to obtain a new lease.

From his brother William's will we gather that John married, and had a daughter named Anne, who became the wife of one of the Hide family. There is nothing to show that John left his native county, or settled in Ireland.

Richard Poe, the fourth son of Anthony Poe, of Papplewick, is only known to us from his father's will. Richard was one of the ordinary Christian names in the family, having its origin, no doubt, with Richard Poe, of Poesfeld, Derbyshire. It was given by Thomas Poe, the third son of Anthony Poe, to his eldest son, and was also borne by the Under-Keeper of Sherwood Forest.

Edward Poe, named in the Ulster Muster Roll of 1630, was, of course, some relation of Anthony Poe and his brothers. An Edward Poe, of Gedling, in Nottinghamshire, is mentioned in the bill filed by Simon Poe, senior, on the 1st May, 1668, referred to at p. 5, *ante.*

On the 17th April, 1662, Anne Poe, of Killnegurdon (now Killygordon), County Donegal, filed a bill in the Court of Chancery in Ireland against Ralph Mansfield and others ; and from the statements in the bill it appears that she was a daughter of John Mansfield, and a granddaughter of Ralph

Mansfield, the elder, both of Killnegurdon, and that on the occasion of her marriage with Robert Goodwin, her first husband, a provision had been made for her by her grandfather out of the Killnegurdon estate, which she now sought to enforce. After Robert Goodwin's death, she married a Mr. Poe; but his Christian name is not mentioned in the proceedings, and he had died before the institution of the suit. Possibly he may have been the Edward Poe above referred to; or if John Poe came to Ireland, this lady may have been his wife, and the mother of his daughter, Ann Hide. But we have nothing to assist us in any conjectures on the subject.

VIII.

EDGAR ALLAN POE : HIS ANCESTRY : STATEMENTS OF HIS
BIOGRAPHERS : DIFFICULTIES IN CONNECTING THE POES
OF THE COUNTY CAVAN WITH OTHER IRISH POES : POES
OF PARISH OF CLONFEACLE : POWELL FAMILY OF COUNTY
ARMAGH : TRUE ANCESTRY OF EDGAR ALLAN POE.

A GENEALOGICAL problem of great interest connected with Irish
Poes has hitherto remained unsolved. Edgar Allan Poe, the
famous American poet and writer, was undoubtedly descended
from John Poe, of Dring, in the Parish of Kildallon and County
Cavan, who emigrated to Pennsylvania about the year 1749 or
1750, with his wife, and such of his children as were then born.

His wife was Jane McBride, who is believed to have been a
daughter of the Rev. Robert McBride, of Ballymoney, County
Antrim, Presbyterian minister, and a sister of John McBride, who
entered the British Navy as an A.B., but rose eventually to the
rank of Admiral.

The father of this John Poe was David Poe, also of Dring,
who appears to have been a tenant-farmer in fairly comfortable
circumstances, but probably a man without much education. In
the old vestry book of Kildallon Parish he is mentioned in
1720, 1724, 1725, 1726, and 1731 as one of the overseers of roads
in the parish ; and in the minutes of the 12th April, 1726, he
signs his name as " David Pooe (*sic*)." The signature " David
Poe " is one of those affixed to the minutes of the vestry meetings
of 1725 and 1732, but is obviously in the handwriting of the
rector of the parish, the Rev. James Brabazon, who also appears
to have signed the name " David Pooe " to the minutes of the
vestry held on the 5th October, 1731.[1]

On the 31st October, 1741, David Poe and his son John,
described both as of " Drin," entered into the customary bond to

---

[1] The Rev. Robert Leech, Rector of Drumlane, Co. Cavan, has kindly
allowed me to inspect and take extracts from this Vestry Book.—E. T. B.

the Bishop of Clogher on the issue of a licence to solemnize matrimony between John Poe, of the Parish of Kildallon and Diocese of Kilmore, and Jane McBride, of the Parish of Drumully, which was in the Diocese of Clogher and County of Feimanagh

The signatures of both father and son to this document suggest that the writing even of their names was a trouble to them.[1]

The marriage was solemnized shortly afterwards; and, under an agreement then made, John Poe was put in possession of one-third of his father's farm.

David Poe made his will, dated the 25th August, 1742. He was therein described as of Dring, in the Parish of Kildallon and County of Cavan, farmer; and he thereby bequeathed to his wife, together with his son-in-law, Archibald Scott, and Anne Scott, his wife, the one-half of his holding, being a fourth part of Dring, together with all movables then in his possession: and secondly to his son Alexander, the sum of £5 sterling, in case he came to this country within six years next after the testator's decease. He gave £3 to Mary Cowan; and to his son John he gave, together with the third he then enjoyed by marriage article, as much of the testator's holding as would make up the half, being the fourth part of Dring, together with ten head of sheep and the one-half of all tackling belonging to the plough; and he further exempted him from all rent theretofore (due), and so to continue until the first day of May next ensuing the date of his will; and he appointed his wife sole executrix.[2] The will was signed by the testator meiely by a mark.

David Poe died in the course of the following year, and on 22nd September, 1742, his will was proved in the Consistorial Court of Kilmore, by his widow, Sarah Poe, the executrix named in the will.

The entire townland of Dring at the present time contains 180a. 3r. 19p. statute measure, of which 12a. 2r. 37p are under water. Consequently, if David Poe's farm only contained a

---

[1] Original bond amongst the documents from the Consistorial Court of Clogher, in the Public Record Office, Dublin.

[2] Original will amongst the documents from the Consistorial Court of Kilmore, in the Public Record Office, Dublin.

moiety of Dring, John Poe's share after his father's death would not have comprised more than about 42a. of arable land.

After his marriage he seems to have been a member of the Presbyterian Congregation worshipping at Croghan, which is situate near the town of Killeshandra, and about three and a-half miles from Dring.

The old baptismal and marriage register[1] of this Congregation is still extant; and although some pages at the commencement of the baptismal portion of it have fallen out, three Poe baptisms are still to be found in it, and are, no doubt, those of three of the children of John and Jane Poe.

The following are the entries :—

> " 1744 : 31st July, George Poo " (*sic*).
> " 1745/6 : 19th March, Mary Poo " (*sic*).
> " 1747/8 : 16th February, Jean Poo " (*sic*).

Under the date of 20th September, 1745, there is the entry of the baptism of Archibald Scott, who was probably a child of John Poe's sister, Anne Scott, and her husband, Archibald Scott.

There were ten children issue of the marriage of John Poe and Jane McBride, and of these David was the eldest. But the entry of his baptism would have appeared on one of the pages of the Croghan register that is now missing. As no Poe baptismal entries appear in the register after February 1748/9, we may conclude that the emigration of John Poe with his wife and children to Pennsylvania took place about 1749 or 1750.

The descent of Edgar Allan Poe from David Poe, of Dring, is shown in the following table :—

---

[1] I am much indebted to the Rev. J. II. Whitsitt, the Minister of Killeshandra Congregation, for permitting me to inspect and take extracts from this interesting old register.—E. T. B.

E

DAVID POE, = SARAH ——.
of Dring, Co. Cavan,
farmer.

Will, 25 Aug., 1742;
pr. 22 Sept., 1742.

JOHN POE, = JANE,
of Dring, Co Cavan,   dau. of (Rev. Robt)
and afterwards of   McBride;
Pennsylvania,   m. Sept., 1741;
d. circa 1756.   d. 1802

ALEXANDER POE, =
emigrated to
America.

ANNE,
m. Archibald Scott

WILLIAM POE, = FRANCES,
moved to   dau. of — Winslow.
Georgia, 1802;
d. Aug., 1805

Other
children.

DAVID POE, = ELIZABETH,
Deputy-Assistant   dau. of — Carnes,
Quartermaster-General of Pennsylvania;
in Revolutionary Army. d. 7 July, 1835.
Moved to Baltimore,
1776; d. 17 Oct., 1816.

GEORGE POE, = KATHERINE,
bapt. 31 July, 1744.   dau. of — Dawson.

DAVID POE, = ELIZABETH,
b. 1786;   dau of — Arnold, and
d. 1811.   widow of C. D. Hopkins;
              m. 1805;
              d. 8 Dec., 1811.

MARIA,
b. 12 March, 1790;
m. 13 July, 1817,
William Clemm;
d 16 Feb., 1871.

Other
children.

WILLIAM HENRY LEONARD POE,
b. Feb., 1807;
d. July, 1831.

EDGAR ALLAN POE, = VIRGINIA,
b. 19 Jan., 1809;   dau. of William Clemm,
d.s.p. 7 Oct., 1849.   by his wife, Maria Poe;
                       b. Aug., 1822;
                       m. 16 May, 1836;
                       d. 30 Jan., 1847.

ROSALIE,
b. 1810;
d. 21 July, 1874.

The first mention that has been found of David Poe, the eldest son of John and Jane Poe, represents him as a wheel-wright; but he engaged in some other business on moving to Baltimore, and seems to have been successful in it.

On the outbreak of the War of Independence he warmly and actively supported the American cause, and from his excellent business qualities was appointed in September, 1779, Deputy-Assistant Quartermaster-General on the Baltimore lines. From holding this post he was afterwards known in the family as "General Poe." He gained the confidence and esteem of Lafayette, who remained his life-long friend.

His eldest son, David, was trained for the law; but he married Mrs. Elizabeth Hopkins, an actress, and went on the stage. "General" Poe and the other members of his family were strict Presbyterians; and this marriage, and the adoption of the profession of an actor by his eldest son, were a great grief to the General, and caused an estrangement between him and his son.

Edgar Allan Poe was the second son of the marriage of David Poe and Elizabeth Hopkins, *née* Arnold; and for the career and works of this gifted but unfortunate genius, reference should be made to the Encyclopædias, or to some of the numerous books that deal with his life and writings.

The romance associated with the writings of Edgar Allan Poe has, unfortunately, been imported by many of his biographers into their account of his ancestry. For this Mrs. Sarah Helen Whitman—who was at one time engaged to be married to the poet—is to a large extent responsible.

In her little book on "Edgar Poe and his Critics," published in New York in 1860, she states :—

> "Those who are curious in tracing the effects of country and lineage in the mental and constitutional peculiarities of men of genius may be interested in such facts as we have been enabled to gather in relation to the ancestry of the poet. The awakening interest in genealogical researches will make these acceptable to many readers ; and in their possible influence on a character so anomalous as that of Edgar Poe they are certainly worthy of note.
>
> "John Poe, the great-grandfather of Edgar Poe, left Ireland for America about the middle of the last century. He was of the old Norman family of Le Poer, a name conspicuous in Irish history. Sir Roger Le Poer went to Ireland, as Marshal to Prince John, in

the reign of Henry II, and became the founder of a race connected with some of the most romantic incidents of Irish history.

. . . .

"The family of the Le Poers, like that of the Geraldines and other Anglo-Norman settlers in Ireland, passed from Italy into the north of France, and from France through England and Wales into Ireland, where, from their isolated position and other causes, they retained for a long period their hereditary traits, with far less modification from intermarriage or consociation with other races than did their English compeers. Meantime the name underwent various changes in accent and orthography. A few branches of the family still bore in Ireland the old Italian name of De la Poe.

"John Poe, the great-grandfather of Edgar Poe, married a daughter of Admiral McBride, distinguished for his naval achievements, and connected with some of the most illustrious families of England. From genealogical records, transmitted by him to his son, David Poe, the grandfather of the poet, who was but two years of age when his parents left Ireland, it appears that different modes of spelling the name were adopted by different members of the same family. David Poe was accustomed to speak of the Chevalier le Poer, a friend of the Marquis of Grammont, as having been of his father's family."

In "The Works of Edgar Allan Poe" (Edinburgh, 1874), edited by Mr. John H. Ingram, a memoir of the poet is given, in which the account of his ancestry is founded on Mrs. Whitman's statements. The march of the family from Italy into the North of France, and from France through England and Wales into Ireland, is retold, and—improving on Mrs. Whitman—it is alleged that a few branches of the family *still* bear in Ireland "the old Italian name of De la Poe." It is further stated that through her father, Edward Power, Lady Blessington claimed descent from the same old family.

"A descendant of this famous and high-spirited race was John Poe, who, by his marriage with Jane, daughter of the distinguished naval hero, Admiral McBride, became allied with some of the most illustrious families of Great Britain."

Mr. Richard H. Stoddard edited an edition of "The Works of Edgar Allan Poe" (London, 1896); and in his notice of Poe's ancestry he states[1].—

"This family, which was called De la Poe, must have been very

---

[1] Vol. i, p. 2.

old, if it be true, as we are assured it was, that the name antedated the river Po."

And, after describing the change of name to le Poer, and the settlement of le Poers in Ireland, he proceeds :—

> "It was involved in the internal dissensions of Ireland at a later period ; and when that unfortunate country was invaded by Cromwell, in 1649, only one of its three leading branches escaped his vengeance. Its name gradually changed, as I have remarked, De la Poe becoming le Poer, and Le Poer, Power and Poe ; and with its change of name there was a change of its employments : the marshals and seneschals of old time subsiding in the last century into a country gentleman, who was the father of Lady Blessington ; of an attorney, who wrote the song of Gramachree ('As down on Banna's banks I strayed'); and a certain Mr. John Poe, whose only claim to remembrance is that he was the great-grandfather of Edgar Allan Poe."

In "The Life of Edgar Allan Poe," by Colonel John A. Joyce (New York and London, 1901), we read :—

> "Sir Roger de la Poe, of Italy, accompanied Prince John into Ireland in the year 1185, and the la Poer, Poe, or Power family continued to flourish in the Emerald Isle until a Roundhead Rough-Rider, named Oliver Cromwell, in 1649, ripped up the rebellious Roman Catholics, and crushed their civil and religious rights under the iron heel of despotism, murder, and robbery, in the name of God. It still proceeds.
>
> "John Poe, the father of Lady Blessington, and great-grandfather of Edgar Allan Poe, suffered by the Puritan inundation.
>
> "David Poe, born in Londonderry, the grandfather of the poet, married the daughter of John MacBride, Scotch-Irish Admiral of the Blue. He emigrated to Pennsylvania before our Revolutionary War, and was a wheelwright by trade, and worked at his business in Baltimore, being a leader among the labour fraternities in that city."

All these accounts of Edgar Allan Poe's ancestry might be described in Colonel Joyce's alliterative style as "romance run riot"; but in Mrs. Whitman's case there is the mitigating circumstance that she was dominated by the personality of Poe, and fascinated by the glamour of his genius.

The other biographers, however, might have been expected to write more soberly, and to investigate the alleged matters of fact, before committing themselves to statements that not only lacked evidence to support them, but were demonstrably impossible, or absurd.

Mr. Stoddard must have been laughing in his sleeve when he gravely stated that it was asserted that the family antedated the river Po, as every schoolboy knows that the name of the river in ancient times was Padus, and that Po is but the modern form of the name.

As a very large number of surnames are derived from place-names, a family, illustrious or otherwise, might have acquired its name from the river after it had become known as the Po; but, unfortunately, the name of the river is masculine in Italian—il Po—and the surname of De la Po could not have been derived from it.

As a matter of fact, however, there is no trace of any family of De la Po or De la Poe having ever existed in Italy or France, or *anywhere else*; and if there had been such, on no rational principles could the name have been converted into De la Poer or le Poer, on a migration of the family to France.

The tacking on of the letter *r* to words ending in a vowel, and the pronunciation of "villa" and "sofa" as "villar" and "sofar" are essentially English and American vulgarisms.

That members of a distinguished family called le Poer passed from Normandy to England, and subsequently from England to Ireland, is beyond question. But, as has been pointed out more than once by eminent genealogists, "Le Poer," in its origin, was a purely personal surname,[1] and, perhaps, was a form of "Le Pohier," *i.e.* "the native of Poix"; and *De la* Poer is an absolutely impossible name to have arisen naturally.

In Ireland "le Poer" was gradually changed into "Poore" and "Power"; and had not a member of the Power family by an unfortunate blunder assumed the title of "Count *de la Poer*," on being created a Count of the Holy Roman Empire, the name of De la Poer would never have been heard of. But in law he was of course entitled to take any surname he thought fit.

There is not a tittle of evidence, however, that any member of the Poe family was descended from any le Poer or Power; and the statement as to the identity of the families is without the

---

[1] "The Genealogist," N. S., xii, pp. 215, 221; xiii, pp. 15, 131. "Studies in Peerage and Family History," by J. Horace Round, p. 18.

slightest foundation. But the most ridiculous and audacious assertion made by any of Edgar Allan Poe's biographers is the alleged relationship of the poet's great-grandfather, John Poe, to "the gorgeous" Lady Blessington. According to Mr. Stoddard, she was a sister of John Poe; while Colonel Joyce represents her as his daughter.

This is a matter whose absurdity could at once have been made manifest if these biographers had taken the trouble to investigate the parentage of Lady Blessington, and the date of her birth. Marguerite Power, who by her second marriage became Lady Blessington, was the second daughter of Edmund Power, a small Roman Catholic landowner in the County Tipperary, by his wife, Ellen Sheehy, who was also a member of the same Church. The future Lady Blessington was born at Knockbrit, near Clonmel, County Tipperary, on the 1st September, 1789—that is to say, nearly half a century after John Poe's marriage with Jane McBride, and about thirty-three years after his death. The grim Presbyterian farmer would turn in his grave if he learned that this brilliant and fashionable lady—the child of Roman Catholic parents, and the subject of many scandals—had been represented as his sister or daughter; and if he were capable of feeling amused, he would surely grin at hearing that he had been described as a sufferer from the Puritan inundation of Ireland, and a victim to Oliver Cromwell's despotism.

A statement by Poe's biographers as to the parentage of Jane McBride, the wife of John Poe, also needs correction.

Admiral John McBride was the younger brother of Dr. David McBride, who was born on 26th April, 1726. He could not have been more than fourteen years of age when John Poe was married, and, therefore, it is impossible that Jane McBride could have been his daughter. It is now, however, alleged that she was his sister, and a daughter of the Rev. Robert McBride, Presbyterian Minister at Ballymoney. This is possible; but the Rev. Robert McBride was a man of strong views, and it is difficult to understand how his daughter came to be married in the Parish Church of Drumully, County Fermanagh, under a licence granted by the Bishop of Clogher, and not in her father's meeting-house at Ballymoney, County Antrim.

With respect to Edgar Allan Poe's biographer, Mr. John H.

Ingram, it is right to say that in his later book, " Edgar Allan
Poe: His Life, Letters, and Opinions " (London, 1880),[1] he
abandons Mrs. Whitman's ideas as to Poe's ancestry, and
states :—

> " It must be confessed that the earlier reliable records do not
> carry the paternal ancestry of Edgar Allan Poe further back than
> the middle of the last century; but if his ancestors were descended,
> as is extremely possible, from the Poës of Riverston (Co. Tipperary,
> Ireland), the race may be traced back nearly two centuries earlier."

Mr. James A. Harrison—Edgar Allan Poe's most recent
biographer—in his "Life and Letters of Edgar Allan Poe" (New
York, 1902 and 1903), has also taken a sensible view of Poe's
ancestry.   He states :—

> " The biographers of Poe are indebted to Mr. John H Ingram
> for the surest testimony, obtained from the poet's family in Baltimore,
> as to his ancestry.
> " 'There is no good reason,' says John P. Poe, Esq., of Baltimore,
> ' to suppose that the ancestors of Edgar Allan Poe were descended
> from the Le Poers [the Anglo-Norman family who passed from Italy
> to France, and from France to England, Wales, and Ireland, and
> with whom Mrs. Sarah Helen Whitman, the poet's *fiancée*, in 1848,
> connected her own and Poe's progenitors].   John Poe, the progeni-
> tor of the family in America, emigrated from the north of Ireland a
> number of years before the Revolution, and purchased a farm in
> Lancaster County, Pennsylvania, whence he afterwards removed to
> Cecil County, Maryland.   At the time of the Revolution he was
> residing in Baltimore.   His wife was Jane M'Bride, believed to be a
> sister [not a daughter, as frequently stated] of James M'Bride,
> Admiral of the Blue, and M.P. for Plymouth in 1785.' "

That David Poe, of Dring, was a descendant of one of the
Poes who settled in Ireland in connexion with the Plantation
of Ulster is a most natural and reasonable supposition ; but
when an attempt is made to trace the descent, great difficulties
present themselves.   In the first place, there is a total absence
of any evidence on the subject.   Inquiries from the land-agent
of Lord Farnham, on whose estate the farm of Dring is situate,
have elicited that the rentals of David Poe's time—which might
have thrown some light on the matter—are not forthcoming.
The farm was probably held under a tenancy from year to

---

[1] Vol. ii, App. A, p. 248.

year, and no deed or other instrument dealing with it was
registered in the Registry of Deeds Office. The old parish
registers of Kildallon have long since disappeared, and there
are not any old Presbyterian registers in the County Cavan,
other than that of Croghan, already referred to. Furthermore,
a Hearth-money Roll of the County Cavan of the year
1664, which gives the names of all the householders in the
county at that date, down to the occupier of the humblest
cottage, does not contain the name of Poe. But, independently
of the failure of proof, there are difficulties of a different nature.
From which of the original settlers should descent be traced?
Major William Poe may be disregarded, as the terms of his will
negative the idea of his having left male descendants. Lieutenant Thomas Poe seems also out of the question, as we have—
as will be seen by Pedigrees A and B—very full information as
to his sons and their issue. The descendants of Captain
Anthony Poe's elder son, Samuel Poe, contemporaneous with
David Poe, of Dring, have been traced; and as to Anthony Poe,
the younger son of Captain Anthony Poe, the absence of any
reference to him in the will of Major William Poe, by which
small legacies were bequeathed to his brother and sisters,
suggests that he was then dead. He was an infant at the date
of his father's will, and we have no subsequent mention of him
in any document. Besides, it must be borne in mind that the
sons and grandsons of Lieutenant Thomas Poe and Captain
Anthony Poe were in quite a different social position from
David Poe, of Dring—a circumstance not to be lost sight of at
times in genealogical investigations. Either John Poe or Edward
Poe would then remain as a possible ancestor; and as Major
William Poe seems to have been desirous to include all his
nephews and nieces in his diminutive legacies, and only mentions
a daughter of his brother John, there is a presumption—slight
perhaps—that John had not any son. Moreover, we have no
reason to believe that John ever settled in Ireland. As to
Edward, all that can be said of him is that, after his appearance
with sword and pike at the Muster of 1630, he vanishes from the
scene. But another difficulty arises from the fact that "David,"
which occurs three times as a baptismal name amongst Edgar
Allan Poe's ancestors, is not found elsewhere in the Poe family.

Under these circumstances it occurred to the present writer

to make a careful investigation as to whether there had been in Ireland any other *unattached* Poes—if that expression may be used.

An administration bond, found amongst the records of the Diocese of Armagh, in the Public Record Office, Dublin, dated 5th February, 1764, and entered into by Grace Poe, widow of Thomas Poe, late of Drummond, in the Parish of Clonfeacle, County Tyrone, farmer, on obtaining letters of administration of the effects of her deceased husband, led to an examination of the Parish Registers of the Parish of Clonfeacle. Clonfeacle is a large parish, situate partly in the Barony of Oneiland West, and County Armagh, but chiefly in the Barony of Dungannon, and County Tyrone. Amongst the townlands in the Tyrone portion of the parish are Drummond (called in some documents Drummon and Drummin), and Ballymackleduff, otherwise Ballymuckleduff, which almost adjoins Drummond.

The Parish Registers go back to a much earlier date than is ordinarily found in country Parish Registers in Ireland. The Register of Baptisms begins in 1743; but both in it and in the Register of Burials there are at times serious gaps.

The earliest entry in the Registers relating to a Poe is as follows :—

> " Jan. 4, 1761.
> " Then was married, by the Rev. Mr. James Dobbins, Thomas Poe and Grace MacAtegart, of Drummond."

This, of course, was the Thomas Poe, of Drummond, whose widow, Grace, obtained letters of administration in 1764; and as an Owen *McAtaggart*, of the Parish of Clonfeacle, joined her in the administration bond, " McAtaggart" was probably the correct rendering of her maiden name. We next find from the Registers, that James Henderson and Jane Poe, of Ballymuckleduff, were married by licence on 7th April, 1809, and that John Kerr and Mary Poe were married by licence on 15th July, 1814. On the 19th March, 1820, Thomas, son of William Poe, of Ballymuckleduff, was baptized, and on the 26th July, 1825, there is an entry of the baptism of William, son of William and Sarah Poe, of Ballymuckleduff.

In 1822, the curate of the Parish of Clonfeacle made a house-to-house visitation of the parish, and took a census of all who were attendants at the Parish Church, recording the particulars afterwards in the Parish Register. Amongst those in the townland of Ballymuckleduff (which is described as part of the estate of Lord Powerscourt) appear :—" William Poe and wife and one child—two communicants," to which the curate has added—" Offended with the Rector."

These were William and Sarah Poe, and the youthful Thomas Poe, who had been baptized on 19th March, 1820.

On 10th April, 1857, is entered the burial of William Poe, of Ballymuckleduff, aged seventy-five.

This information gathered from the Parish Registers may be supplemented by the following marriage licence bonds amongst the records of the Diocese of Armagh :—

Bond, dated 27th June, 1782, by John Poe, of Drummond, Parish of Clonfeacle, and County Tyrone, shoemaker, and John Waugh, of Ballymuckleduff, Parish of Clonfeacle, weaver, on the issue of a licence to solemnize matrimony between John Poe and Isabella Williams, of Drummond, spinster.

Bond, dated 13th April, 1841, by John Briars, of Kilmore, in the Parish of Aghaloo, and County Tyrone, and William Poe, of Ballymackleduff, in the Parish of Clonfeacle, and County Tyrone, farmers, on the issue of a licence for the marriage of John Briars and Jane Poe, of Ballymackleduff, spinster.

From these materials the following conjectural pedigree of the Poes of the Parish of Clonfeacle might be sketched out ·—

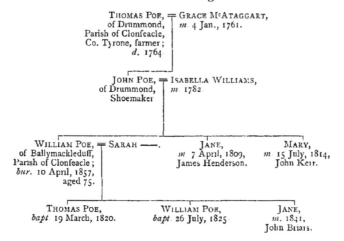

THOMAS POE, = GRACE McATAGGART,
of Drummond, | *m* 4 Jan., 1761.
Parish of Clonfeacle,
Co. Tyrone, farmer;
d. 1764

JOHN POE, = ISABELLA WILLIAMS,
of Drummond, | *m* 1782
Shoemaker

WILLIAM POE, = SARAH ——.   JANE,   MARY,
of Ballymackleduff, | *m* 7 April, 1809,   *m* 15 July, 1814,
Parish of Clonfeacle; | James Henderson.   John Keir.
bur. 10 April, 1857,
aged 75.

THOMAS POE,   WILLIAM POE,   JANE,
bapt 19 March, 1820.   *bapt* 26 July, 1825.   *m.* 1841,
John Briars.

There is also a marriage licence bond amongst the Armagh
Diocesan Records, dated 18th December, 1836, entered into by
Thomas Poe, of Drummond, in the Parish of Clonfeacle, and
John Burgess, of Finlay, in the same parish, on the issue of a
licence to solemnize matrimony between Thomas Poe and Susan
Burgess, of Finlay, spinster; and this Thomas Poe might be
tacked on tentatively to the foregoing pedigree as a grandson
of Thomas Poe, and Grace, his wife, by a younger son of
theirs.[1]

However, for the present purpose, it is enough to state that
for what is substantially a century, *i.e.*, from the marriage of
Thomas Poe, of Drummond, and Grace McAtaggart, in 1761,
to the burial of William Poe, of Ballymackleduff, in 1857, a
number of persons bearing the name of Poe lived in the Parish
of Clonfeacle, County Tyrone, whose connexion with Major
William Poe, or one of his brothers, has not been made out.
But it may also be added that the Poes of Dring, County
Cavan, and the Poes of Clonfeacle, County Tyrone, are the *only*
Poes in Ireland hitherto noticed in the Public Records of whom
such a statement can be made.

Whence, then, did these Poes come? They did not spring
from the ground in a night, like mushrooms; and, at a time
when travelling was difficult and costly, they are not likely
to have migrated to these inland localities from any great
distance.

The Hearth-money Rolls of Tyrone, for 1665 and 1666, and
many Subsidy Rolls of earlier date have been examined, and
no Poe has been found in them. The Hearth-money Rolls
of about the same period for the counties which surround
Tyrone, viz., Monaghan, Fermanagh, Donegal, Londonderry,
and Armagh, have also been examined, but with a like negative
result. The Cavan Hearth-money Roll, as already stated, does
not contain any Poe; and that for Louth only records the
presence in the county of Mary Poe, the widow of Captain
Anthony Poe.

So far, the quest for *unattached* Poes had given no assistance
towards solving the problem of the ancestry of David Poe, of

---

[1] The pedigree is not a correct one, but such as might have been
suggested from the materials stated.

Dring; but, on the contrary, had evolved another puzzle of great difficulty as to the origin of the Poes of Clonfeacle. It seemed, indeed, a case of attempting to explain *obscurum per obscurius.*

But light came from an unexpected quarter, and not only was the cloud of mystery that seemed to surround the Clonfeacle Poes dispelled, but a clue was seen to the discovery of the solution of the original problem.

An examination was made of the returns for the Parish of Clonfeacle of the Census taken in Ireland in 1821—which, it will be remembered, was the year after the baptism of Thomas, son of William Poe, of Ballymackleduff, and the year before the curate of Clonfeacle had taken his census of the Church population—and not a single Poe was found within the limits of the parish !

But the returns disclosed that there were a large number of *Powells* in this parish ; and after a few minutes' consideration, it became manifest that those in the townlands of Drummond and Ballymuckleduff included persons who have been already referred to as *Poes.*

These two townlands were thickly inhabited, and the whole population practically was engaged in hand-loom weaving and spinning, in connexion with the linen manufacture.

In Drummond there were three families of Powells, and in Ballymuckleduff three more, with the addition of a mother-in-law Powell, quartered in the house of a son-in-law named White.

In Ballymuckleduff the inhabitants of one house were returned thus :—

> " William Powell, aged 34, farmer.
> Sarah Powell, wife, aged 27, flax spinner.
> Thomas Powell, son, aged 1.
> Elizabeth Carter, aged 25, flax spinner, servant."

There are, of course, the " William Poe and wife and one child " mentioned in the Curate's Census of 1822; the " William and Sarah Poe," whose son William was baptized on the 26th July, 1825 ; the " William Poe," whose burial at the age of seventy-five is recorded in the Parish Register, under the date of the 10th April, 1857 ; and " Thomas, son of William Poe, of Ballymuckleduff," baptized on the 19th March, 1820.

In Drummond we find living in one house .—

> " John Powell, aged 64, farmer.
> Isabella Powell, wife, aged 54, flax spinner.
> Anne Powell, daughter, aged 17, flax spinner.
> Richard Powell, son, aged 13, linen weaver.
> Thomas Powell, son, aged 20, linen weaver.
> Margaret Powell, son's wife, aged 21, flax spinner."

This was " John Poe, of Drummond," who was a party to the marriage licence bond, dated 27th June, 1782, executed on obtaining a licence for his marriage with Isabella Williams. The latter, after the manner of her kind, seems to have dropped some years from her age in the Census return.

In the Census Returns of 1831, we find all the Powells in Drummond and Ballymuckleduff appearing as *Poels.* These returns are not so satisfactory as those of 1821, as the names of only heads of families are given, and ages are not stated.

However, in Ballymackleduff, we have " William Poel," with three males and four females in his household ; and this must have been " William Poe," husband of Sarah Poe, and father of Thomas and William Poe.

In Upper Drummond appear " John Poel " and " Thomas Poel " as separate householders, and these were, without doubt, identical with " John Poe," the husband of Isabella Williams, and their son " Thomas Poe."

In the Census Returns of 1841, for the Parish of Clonfeacle and townland of Ballymackleduff, we again meet with William Powell and his family—the " William Poe " of the Curate's Census in 1822. The enumerator had indorsed the Census paper for " William Poel," but the head of the family signs it as " William Powel." The following are the particulars :—

> " William Powel, aged 50, mar. 1819, farmer.
> Sarah Powel, aged 40, wife, mar. 1819.
> Thomas Powel, aged 20, son.
> Mary Jane Powel, aged 17, daughter.
> Catherine Anne Powel, aged 10, daughter.
> Maria Powel, aged 6, daughter.
> William Powel, aged 14, son."

Two other families in the same townland also bear the name of Powel.

In the townland of Drummond one Census return is indorsed John Powell, and three other returns are indorsed respectively Richard *Poe*, William *Poe*, and Thomas *Poe*; but in each of the four returns the surname is given as "Powel," though in the case of William Poe the signature attached is "William Poel." The indorsements, however, afford the strongest evidence that amongst their neighbours Richard, William, and Thomas Powell were known as Poes. This William Poe, or Poel, was a son of "John Poe of Drummond," who executed the bond of 27th June, 1782, when obtaining a licence for his marriage with Isabella Williams; and the return gives the following particulars :—

"William Powel, aged 40, widower, mar. 1818, farmer.
John Powel,[1] aged 86, father, mar. 1783.
Isabela Powel, aged 80, wife, mar. 1783, spinner.
James Powel, aged 20, son.
Isabela Powel, aged 14, daughter.
Ann Powel, aged 11, daughter.
Mary Powel, aged 9, daughter.
Eliza Powel, aged 5, daughter."

When the Census of 1851 was taken, great changes had come over the country. The famine of 1846–1847 had led to extensive emigration, and the hand-loom weaving carried on in the farm-houses and cottages in the North of Ireland had to a large extent been supplanted by great spinning-mills and factories.

The Census returns show great changes in the population of the Parish of Clonfeacle. In the townland of Drummond not a single Powell, Poel, or Poe is to be found.

In Ballymackleduff William Powell, Poel, or Poe, and his family alone remain.

The Census return in his case is as follows :—

"William Poel, aged 50, mar. 1820, farmer.
Sarah Poel, aged 49, wife, mar. 1820.
Thomas Poel, aged 28, son, farmer.
William Poel, aged 26, son, labourer.
Mary Jane Poel, aged 24, daughter.
Thomas Briars, aged 8, grandson."
With the addition of two servants.

---

[1] John Powel and his wife, Isabella, were members of the Society of Friends, and their deaths, in 1845 and 1844, are recorded in the Registers of the Monthly Meeting of Grange, County Tyrone. The same Registers

And the Census return is signed by the head of the family as "William *Pole*."

From all this we gather that "Poel" and "Pole" were variants of the surname "Powell," and that for a century, if not longer, "Poe" was a well-known abbreviated form of the name in this part of Ireland.

Going back now with the knowledge thus acquired, we find this corroborated in many ways. Thomas Poe, of Drummond, who was married to Grace McAtaggart, on 4th January, 1761, obtained the marriage licence by virtue of a bond, dated 4th December, 1760, made out in the name of "Thomas Powell," and signed by him as "Thomas Pooel." A will of John Poell, of Drummond (father of John Poe, who married Isabella Williams), dated 2nd October, 1781, bears the signature of "John Poole"; and the marriage licence bond, dated 13th April, 1841, already mentioned, executed on the issue of a licence for the marriage of John Briars with Jane Poe, daughter of William Poe, of Ballymackleduff, is signed by the latter "*William Pul.*" But, on the other hand, the marriage licence bond, dated 27th June, 1782, entered into on the issue of the licence for the marriage of John Poe, of Drummond, and Isabella Williams, bears the signature "John Poe"; and the marriage licence bond of the 18th December, 1836, executed before the marriage of Thomas Poe, of Drummond, and Susan Burgess, is signed "Thomas Poe."

It is quite clear, therefore, that several of the Northern Powells were baptized, married, and buried under the name of Poe, and that some of them used that name when executing formal legal documents.

Powell is a name met with in the County Armagh at an early period. "William Powell, of Castlepark, within the honour of Tutberry (Tutbury), in the County of Stafford, Esq."—one of the Equerries of James I—was one of the original undertakers in the Plantation of Ulster, and was granted the great proportion of Ballyworran (now Ballyvoran), containing 2000 acres, situate in the Barony of Oneiland, and County Armagh. He

---

show that a number of other Poels and Powells, who lived at Bally-mackleduff or Drummond between 1754 and 1845, were members of the Society.

disposed of his interest before long to Michael Obbyns ; but
many persons bearing the name of Powell—not necessarily
related to him in any way—settled early in the seventeenth
century as tenants on the Plantation estates in the North of
Ireland This we know from the Muster Roll of Ulster, already
referred to. Powells then appeared armed with swords, pikes,
or other weapons in the newly-created manors in the Counties
of Cavan, Fermanagh, and Armagh ; but when the Rebellion
of 1641 broke out, they were despoiled of their goods, and driven
from their lands, while at least two of their number were
murdered. After the insurrection was suppressed, Powells were
still found in the County Armagh ; but the Hearth-money Rolls
of 1664-1668 of Cavan and Fermanagh show that they had then
disappeared from these counties.

In the Hearth-money Roll of the County Armagh for the
year 1665 Patrick Powell appears at Magherlecoomore, in the
Barony of Oneiland West, and William Powell at Ballymatrons,
in the Barony of Armagh.   In the Hearth-money Roll of the
county for 1664 the latter appears as William *Poole*.

As already stated, part of the Parish of Clonfeacle is in the
Barony of Oneiland West, County Armagh ; and as no persons
with the name of Powell, or any variant of it, appear in the
Parish of Clonfeacle, or anywhere else within the county, in the
Tyrone Hearth-money Rolls of 1665 or 1666, it is obvious that
the Powells who are found there afterwards were a branch of
the County Armagh family.

Amongst the soldiers who served in one of the regiments of
the Parliamentary Army in Ireland in suppressing the Rebellion
of 1641, and thus became entitled to share in the distribution of
the forfeited lands, were *Jonathan Powell* and *David Powell*.
Their names are found in a certificate of the Court of Claims,
dated 2nd January, 1668/9. This dealt with the claims of
Colonel Henry Pritty, Captain Benjamin Barry, and a large
number of officers and soldiers of the same regiment who had
consented that the certificate should be granted to Henry Pritty,
Benjamin Barry, and the well-known Sir William Petty, author
of the Down Survey, and their heirs, in trust for the several
persons therein mentioned according to their respective rights.
Each officer and soldier had received from the authorities a
debenture for his arrears of pay, and was entitled to have the

F

amount satisfied out of the forfeited lands ; but soldiers whose claims were small in amount sold their claims either to their officers or to outside purchasers, and did not actually receive any grant of lands.   In the present case the total amount of the claims certified was £28,913 16s. 9½d., and the proportion of this due to Colonel Henry Pritty was £2604 2s. 1d.; to Jonathan Powell, £11 19s. 4d. ; and to David Powell, £61 8s. 2d.

The lands dealt with by the certificate, out of which the claims were to be satisfied, were situate in the County of Kerry ; and the greater portion of them seems to have been eventually granted to Sir William Petty, the purchaser of the rights of most of the claimants.

On the 7th June, 1693, Jonathan Powell, described as of Ballyaghey, in the County of Armagh, gent., obtained from the Archbishop of Armagh two leases of See lands in the County Armagh, one of which was a renewal of a former lease of the two townlands of Ballymatron Oughtra and Ballymatron Eightra, while the other was a demise of the townlands of Ballaghey, Ballybrolly, and others. The two townlands of Bally-matron were in the occupation of William Powell at the time the Hearth-money Roll for the County Armagh was compiled in 1665 ; and Jonathan Powell was, we may feel sure, a son of William.

This Jonathan Powell left four daughters and no son ; but the line of the family was continued through his brother Arthur Powell, whom we find as a party to several leases and deeds in the early part of the eighteenth century, and who lived at Drumbee, in the Parish of Armagh.

The foregoing facts establish that there was a family named Powell in the County Armagh, in the seventeenth and eighteenth centuries, and that a branch of it penetrated into a portion of the County Tyrone bordering on Armagh, and was there known from time to time as Powell, Poel, Poole, and Poe. The question then suggests itself: Is there evidence that any member of the family migrated to the County Cavan, and to the locality in which David Poe, of Dring, is found ?

An answer to this can be given with certainty.   On the 8th March, 1719, a licence was issued by the Consistorial Court of the Diocese of Kilmore for the marriage of Jonathan Powell, of the Parish of Armagh, and County of Armagh, gentleman, and Margaret Bennett, of the Parish of Drumlane, County Cavan, and Diocese of Kilmore. This Jonathan Powell was, no doubt, a son of Arthur Powell, of Drumbee, and a nephew of Jonathan Powell, of Ballyaghey and Ballybrolly.

After his marriage he moved to Corr, in the Parish of Templeport, County Cavan, which adjoins the Parish of Kildallon, in which the Townland of Dring is situate. It also adjoins the Parish of Drumlane, in which Margaret Bennett had previously resided; and this circumstance was probably not without some effect in leading to the move.

Jonathan Powell, of Corr, made his will, dated the 31st August, 1756; and the provisions of it show that he was a tenant farmer of the same class as David Poe, of Dring, and with about the same moderate amount of education. He refers to his wife —under the name of Margery—and to his four sons, Thomas, Jonathan, William, and Martin; his two unmarried daughters, Margery and Judith, and a married daughter, Elizabeth Graham. A bequest to his three sons, Thomas, Jonathan, and William, of boards, planks, hoops, and joyce (*i.e.,* joists), mentions some of them as having been brought by him "out of the County Armagh," and identifies him as a member of the Armagh family of Powell.

Can there be any reasonable doubt, then, that David Poe, of Dring, was also a member of the Powell family, in whose case a custom had arisen—as with some of the Powells of Clonfeacle— of using the contracted form of the name? The signature—such as it is—appended to the minutes of the vestry meeting of the 12th April, 1726, represents it as " Pooe," while in the marriage licence bond of the 31st October, 1741, it appears as " Poe."

The " David " and " Jonathan," of Dring and Corr, recall to mind the fellow-soldiers, " David Powell " and " Jonathan Powell," of the Certificate of the Court of Claims; and it seems highly probable that David Poe, of Dring, was in fact a brother of Jonathan Powell, of Corr, and another son of Arthur Powell, of Drumbee. In the case of the Clonfeacle family, one brother is met with signing his name as Poe, while another living in the same parish always made use of the original name of Powell.

The Parish Registers of Templeport evidence the continuance of the Powell family in the parish down to 1815, if not later; but, as both of David Poe's sons emigrated to America, the latest references in the Dring locality to his descendants are the entries of the baptisms of John Poe's children in the Register of the Presbyterian Congregation of Croghan.

If the foregoing views are accepted, the remote ancestors of Edgar Allan Poe must be sought for in the Powell family, and probably had their origin in Wales. The surname Powell came from Ap Howell, just as Pritchard came from Ap Richard; Bowen, from Ap Owen; and Pugh and Pue, from Ap Hugh. David, too, is a characteristic Welsh name.

IX.

ARMS OF THE POE FAMILY: FICTITIOUS PEDIGREE OF THE IRISH POES: ORIGIN OF THE POES OF DERBYSHIRE AND NOTTINGHAMSHIRE : CORRECTIONS IN PUBLISHED PEDIGREES OF THE IRISH POES.

THE right of the Poe family to armorial bearings appears to have been recognized by the College of Arms at the death of Dr. Leonard Poe, if not earlier.

The funeral certificate of Dr. Leonard Poe, recorded in the College of Arms, bears emblazoned on it the following coat:—

> ARMS · *Or a fesse between three crescents azure issuing flames proper.*
>
> CREST . *On a wreath of the colours a boar's head couped erect or pierced through by a broken spear argent.*

The bogus or fictitious pedigree of the Irish family of Poe referred to at p. 1, *ante*, is headed :—

> "Brief abstract from Book 862, Royal College of Heraldry, London, of the race of Poe, or, as anciently pronounced, Pau, of the district of Pau, in Germany."

The pedigree-monger seems to have been ignorant even of the proper designation of Heralds' College; and it is not surprising to learn that no such pedigree, and no such book as that referred to, are to be found in the College of Arms, London.

The whole pedigree is a tissue of fabrications, concocted by some imperfectly educated person, who had not read any of the early wills or other documents relating to the family, and whose main object was to invent as many grand relations and connexions as he could manage, without his frauds being detected.

The production is unworthy of serious notice; but as it has apparently been the means of propagating the legend of the German origin of the family, the first portion of it will be cited *verbatim et literatim* :—

> "This ancient Family was of eminent note in the Upper Pala-
> tinate of the Rhine, and traced beyond the time of the Emperor
> Charles V, and it appears, by record of the Aulic Council, that an
> ancestor served with Rudolph, Count of Nassburgh, in the assault
> on Vienna so early as the end of the 12th century.
>
> "In the year 1641 it appears that Thomas and William Poe,
> two brothers, younger sons of Diedricht (*sic*), the second son of
> Ludolph (*sic*), Baron Ecterburgh (*sic*), Count of Poe.[1] Said Thomas
> and William, being of note (*sic*) rank in Continental service in the
> wars, were solicited by the Protector, Oliver Cromwell, to accept of
> the command of two troops, which they served with much *éclat*,
> and, by the roll of Muster also, it appears that they distinguished
> themselves at the Siege of Limerick ; and these services were so
> highly estimated that the following grants in fee and freehold were
> made to Thomas, as follows."

An exaggerated and wholly inaccurate description then follows of the grant made to Thomas Poe under the Cromwellian Settlement ; and this is succeeded by a statement of an alleged grant to William (described as the younger brother of Thomas) of the lands of Rosinaharley (Rosneharley), County Tipperary.

No grant of any lands in Ireland or elsewhere was made by the Crown to William Poe ; and as a matter of fact the lands of Rosneharley came into the possession of the family for the first time in 1728, by a purchase then made by James Poe, a descendant of the original Thomas Poe. But enough has been stated as to this wretched imposture ; and we now turn to matters of more importance.

The discovery that in the Parish of Clonfeacle, County Tyrone, Poe was undoubtedly a variant or abbreviated form of the surname Powell, has naturally suggested that the Poes of Nottinghamshire and Derbyshire may also have derived their name from Powell. A large number of families bearing the name of Powell, and in no way related to one another, had their origin in Wales. As from the Christian names John, William, David, Thomas, and Richard came the surnames Johnson and Jones, Williamson and Williams, Davidson and Davis or Davies,

---

[1] A Polish Count Poe is mentioned in the "Annual Register" of 14th July, 1817, and perhaps this suggested the title to the pedigree-forger.— E. T. B.

Thomson and Thomas, Richardson, Richards, and Pritchard (*i.e.*, Ap Richard), so from Howell came the surnames Powell (*i.e.*, Ap Howell), and Howell. Many of the Welsh Powells passed from Wales into Shropshire, and from thence into Staffordshire and the neighbouring counties. In the course of their migrations variations in their name arose. For example, we find that a will of William *Powle*, of Stafford, was proved in the Consistorial Court of Lichfield, in 1583/4, and a will of John *Powle*, of Kingsbury, Warwickshire, in 1602/3 ; and the records of the Prerogative Court of York contain the will of Anthony *Powle*, of Fenton, in the Parish of Storton, Nottinghamshire, dated 1st October, 1618. This latter will again shows the transition of the name to *Poole* ; for Anthony Powle, the testator, refers to one of his sons as John Poole, and to his other sons as Robert Poule and Edward Poule.

A number of families bearing the name of Poole were established in Derbyshire and Nottinghamshire in the sixteenth and seventeenth centuries ; and although in many cases it was a corruption of the ancient name of De la Pole, there can be but little doubt that in other cases it was but a variant of Powell.

In some instances, however, a tendency was shown to slur the last syllable of Powell ; and we find in the Lichfield Registry the will of John *Powye*, of Barkswell, in Warwickshire, proved in 1536/7, and the will of Anne *Powawe*, of Sponley, County Salop, proved in 1593. As already shown at p. 4, *ante*, the names *Poa* and *Poy* are met with in Nottinghamshire, in 1609, 1611, and 1661.

In some places Poe makes its appearance where Poole had preceded it. Thus, at Wirksworth, in Derbyshire, we find a Robert *Poole* making his will, on 23rd September, 1585, and a John *Poe* obtaining a certificate of innocency, on the 28th August, 1627 ; and in Yorkshire, the Registers of Leeds Parish Church record the burial of Bryan Poole, on 14th March, 1626, and the baptism of Edith, daughter of Bryan *Poe*, on the 10th May, 1637.

Anthony seems to have been a family name amongst the Poes of Nottinghamshire. Anthony Poe, of Papplewick, had a son Anthony ; and Dr. Leonard Poe had a brother Anthony. It would be a natural supposition, therefore, that Anthony Powle, of Fenton, in Nottinghamshire, whose will has been already referred to, may have been related to the Poe family.

Starting then with the indisputable fact that in the Parish of Clonfeacle, County Tyrone, Poole was a variant of Powell, and Poe a contracted form of the name, there appear to be strong reasons for coming to the conclusion that the Poes of Derbyshire and Nottinghamshire were originally a branch of one of the numerous families of Powell that had their origin in Wales

Having regard to the information contained in the foregoing pages, it is hardly necessary to point out that the account of the Poë lineage, as given in "Burke's Landed Gentry of Ireland," needs several corrections.

The legend as to the German origin of the family should be expunged. Dr. Leonard Poe was *not* Physician to Queen Elizabeth. William and Thomas Poe were *not* at the Siege of Limerick, if the siege referred to was that of 1691. William Poe had died in 1678, and Thomas in 1683, both being then very advanced in years.

William Poe did *not* receive from the Crown a grant of lands in Ireland or elsewhere ; nor was any confirmatory grant made either to William or Thomas, in the reign of William III. Thomas Poe was *not* a Captain ; and Richard, and *not* Emmanuel, was his eldest son.

It is hoped that this little book, with the accompanying pedigrees, may be of some use in putting the facts relating to the pedigree and early history of the Poe family in a connected and intelligible form. The later history can be gathered from the pedigrees without any comment.

APPENDICES AND INDEX

APPENDIX A

DR. LEONARD POE AND HIS SON JAMES POE.

THE Funeral Certificate of Dr. Leonard Poe, registered in the College of Arms, London, is headed by an emblazonment of his Arms as already described at p. 69, *ante*.

It then proceeds thus :—

> "The worshipfull Leonard Poe Esquier Doctor of Phisick, Phisitian of the Household in ordinary both to Kinge James and King Charles, the sonne of James Poe, the sonne of Richard Poe of Poesfeld in the countye of Darby, Departed this mortall life the XXVIIth of March 1631, whose body was interred in Christ-Church London the 31 of the said moneth following. He maried Dionisia Da. of . . . Boone of the County of Sussex, by whom he had yssue 3 sonnes and 6 daughters, Leonard Poe eldist sonne, of the age of 30[ty] yeares, James 2[d] sonne, of the age of 28[ty], Theophilus 3[d] sonne, of the age of about 22 yeares, Jane eldist Da. maried to John Hankinson of Totteridge in the County of Hartford, and had yssue 2 sonnes, Leonard and John, both died young. Elizabeth 2[d] Dau. and Mary 3[d] Da. died unmaried. Suzan 4th Da. mar[d] to John Bastwicke Doctor of Phisick, and hath 2 Da[s] Judith and Dionisia. Judith 5 Da. mar[d] to Thomas Grent Doctor of Phisick, Francis 6 Da. mar[d] to David Ramsey, Page of the Bedchamber to King James and King Charles, and hath yssue William and Francis Ramsey. The executor of the last will and testament of the said Mr. Doctor Poe is Mr. James Poe, his 2[d] sonne.
>
> "This Certificate was taken by Samson Lennard Blewmantle to be recorded in the Office of Armes.
>
> "(Signed) JAMES POE."

James Poe, in the information supplied for the preparation of this Certificate, made a bad blunder as to the dates of his father's death and burial. Dr. Leonard Poe's will bears date 18th February, 1630/1, and was proved on the 25th March, 1630/1, *i.e.* according to the then computation of time, on the first day of the year 1631. It is wholly impossible, then, that he can have died on the 27th March, 1631— two days after his will had been proved!

Very probably James Poe did not attend at the College of Arms until many months had elapsed after his father's death, and he then trusted to a very fallible memory for the dates he gave for both death and burial. Unfortunately it is not possible to ascertain the true date of the burial from the records of Christ-Church, Newgate Street, London, as the Parish Registers of this period are not forthcoming, having been destroyed, as is believed, in the Great Fire of London.

There appears to be some doubt as to the true name of James Poe's wife. In the Allegations for Marriage Licences issued from the Faculty Office of the Archbishop of Canterbury at London (Harl. Soc. xxiv., p. 48) we find:—

> "1660 Dec. 28 Thomas Jenner J^r of the Inner Temple Gent. Bach^r, 23, and Anne Poe of St. Edmund the King, Lombard St, London, Sp^r, 22, dau. of James Poe and *Jane* Poe, late of Swindon Hall, par. Kirkby Overblowes, Co. York dec^d; at St Mary Woolchurch, London."

But from "Wotton's Baronetage," vol. iii, part ii, p. 375, we have the following pedigree:—

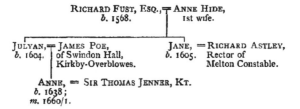

RICHARD FUST, ESQ., = ANNE HIDE, *b.* 1568. — 1st wife.

JULYAN, = JAMES POE, *b.* 1604. — of Swindon Hall, Kirkby-Overblowes.

JANE, = RICHARD ASTLEY, *b.* 1605. — Rector of Melton Constable.

ANNE, = SIR THOMAS JENNER, KT. *b.* 1638; *m.* 1660/1.

And *Julian*, dau. of Richard Fust, Esq., of Hill Court, County Gloucester, is given as the wife of James Poe, of Swindon Hall, in the Lineage of "Jenner of Wenvoe" in "Burke's Landed Gentry."

In the Pedigree of Lowe, of Alderwarley, County Derby ("Jewett's Reliquary," vol. xi, p. 33), we have:—

EDWARD LOWE, = DOROTHY, of Alderwarley, — dau. of Christopher Eyre. living in 1597.

JANE. = JAMES POE, of Co. Derby.

It seems certain, however, that the wife of James Poe, of Swindon Hall (son of Dr. Leonard Poe)—whether her Christian name was Jane or Julian—was a daughter of the above-named Richard Fust; and James Poe who married Jane Lowe must have been some other member of the family.

APPENDIX B

PETITION TO PARLIAMENT OF REDUCED OFFICERS AND SOLDIERS.

THE following petition is taken from a small volume of printed petitions in the British Museum, bearing the press-mark 669 f. 19. This petition, which is No. 59 in the collection, is undated, but in the margin some one has written "December 1654":—

To the Parliament of the Commonwealth of England, Scotland, and Ireland, and Dominions thereunto belonging.

The humble Petition of the Subscribers on the behalf of themselves, and other Reduced Officers and Souldiers therein concerned.

SHEWETH,

That in their zealous and cordial affection to the just rights and freedome of this Nation, with expence of blood and patrimony, they have faithfully served this Common-wealth from the beginning of the late wars until reduced by Order of Parliament, with promise of satisfaction forthwith of such Arrears as were due unto them, which may appear by several Orders and Ordinances of Parliament; and many of them voluntarily since the said reducement, engaged to the hazard of all that was dear unto them for the Public good.

Neverthelesse, their constant expectations (grounded upon the many promises and engagements of the then Supreme Authority of this Nation) have been wholly frustrated, although they (to their great expence) constantly attended with many humble Addresses during the space of seven years past, for the obtaining of their just satisfaction; for want of which, divers are brought to extreme penury, many starved, and others in prison ready to perish.

But their long and tedious attendance producing no fruit from the Parliament, after their dissolution, they then made their humble Addresses to his Highnesse, and Honourable Council, who were pleased to refer their Petition to the Council of the Army, who upon mature consideration and conference had with your Petitioners, returned their sense and results thereon to his Highnesse, and the said Council, by whose Order the same was transmitted (by the hands of Captain Howard) to the late Parliament, who after daily solicitation, did admit them (for satisfaction out of lands in Ireland) into an Act intitled "An Act for satisfaction of Adventurers and Souldiers," dated the twenty-sixt day of September, 1653.

That after the late Parliament dissolved themselves, they then made their humble Addresses to his Highnesse, who was pleased to recommend them and their desires unto the speedy and serious consideration of his Council sitting at White-Hall, in order to their due relief and satisfaction, and perceiving that upon the addresses of some Officers (under the same qualification with your Petitioners) Lands both in England and Ireland have been obtained for their satisfaction; and your Petitioners hitherto (by reason of the great and weighty affairs of the Common-wealth) are unsatisfied, so that your Petitioners upon this account are without hope of reaping any benefit, or to be enabled to receive satisfaction by that security in the said Act, according to the purport and meaning thereof.

Your Petitioners therefore humbly pray that your Honours would be pleased to take the premises into your serious consideration, to the end that as the said Act of the late Parliament intends a security unto them, their interest may be preserved therein; and that some speedy course may be taken for stating the Arrears of such Officers and Souldiers as are not yet stated; and that such whose Arrears are already stated by Committees or Commissioners, or any Authorised by Order or Ordinance of Parliament, having faithfully served this Common-wealth, and no ways forfeited their right to their just dues; All of them or their Assignes may be enabled by bond or otherwise to receive satisfaction for their Arrears so stated, and to be stated, out of such Lands in Ireland as are yet undisposed of (viz.) in the Counties of Dublin, Cork, Kildare, and Caterlagh, or out of such Lands there belonging to Corporations forfeited, or out of Bishops', Dean and Chapter Lands there, or out of Forrests Lands in England yet unsold, or by some such other way as to your grave Judgement shall seem meet, that so your Petitioners may be freed from their tedious and expensive attendance, receive the price of their blood, and be put into a condition to be more instrumentally serviceable for this Common-wealth, which is their desire.

And they shall pray, &c.

Edward Freman, Samuel Carlton, William Poe, William Pickering.
Humphreey Brewster, Edward Hook, Timothy Crusoe, Matthias Nichols.
Nicholas Devereux, Ambrose Tyndale, Leonard Morton, Anthony Poe.
Emanuel Neal, Richard Stephens, John Birkbeck, Richard Griffith.
Walter Bosvile, John Mall, John Rugeley, Edward Harrington, William Tivey, Francis Cotton.

INDEX

OF NAMES OF PERSONS AND PLACES.